J

C000150319

Bratislava

OLD TOWN

Compiled by: Daniel Kollár

BRATISLAVA
OLD TOWN

1st edition, 2005

Author: Ján Lacika
Compiled by: Daniel Kollár
Editors: Daniel Kollár and Peter Augustini
Translation: Hana Contrerasová
Responsible editor: Daniel Kollár
Technical editor: Zuzana Kollárová
Photographs: Ján Lacika, Ivan Kostroň, Slovak National Museum, Gallery of Bratislava, Slovak National Gallery, Archeological Museum, City Museum
Plans and situation maps: Ján Lacika
Fragments of town plan Bratislava: VKÚ, a. s., Harmanec
Illustrated map: Pegas, s. r. o., Považská Bystrica
Design: Ján Hladík
Print: VKÚ, a. s., Harmanec

This book is also available in the Slovak, English, German, Russian, Polish, French, Spanish, and Italian languages.

Any, including partial use of this work is permitted only with the written consent of DAJAMA Publishers.

© DAJAMA, Ľubľanská 2, 831 02 Bratislava, Slovak Republic
Phone/fax: +421 2 4463 1702
info@dajama.sk
www.dajama.sk

ISBN 80-88975-91-3

INTRODUCTION

There are only several cities on the map of Europe with such a unique position and rich history as those of Bratislava. This strategic spot has repeatedly played a vital role in history of central Europe. In Middle Ages it was centre of culture and learning the Kingdom of Hungary it was part of. After Turks penetrated into the country, Bratislava was declared the Capital of the Kingdom and the seat of the Diet, the coronation town of kings and queens of the Kingdom of Hungary. The centre of all important historical events was the Old Town with numerous cultural and historical monuments and interesting architecture. Although Bratislava became a relatively large city with almost half a million inhabitant, its Old Town has kept its intimate nature proper to Central European historic cities.

Dear readers,

This is the tourist guidebook the aim of which is to present Bratislava, especially its Old Town as the highly interesting Central European locality for its history, architecture, culture and arts. It contains the basic characteristics of the past of the city and its most important cultural and historical monuments. The historic centre of Bratislava was given greatest attention. The detailed description of historic streets and squares that formed the skeleton of the medieval town traces the individual monuments and interesting places in form of a walk. The reader only has to stop in front of the particular palace, church or historic house and to read its story. Plans facilitate orientation. The guidebook informs readers about numerous remarkable details hidden in the interior of yards, churches or halls of palaces open to public. The book also contains hints (marked by asterisks) of the most attractive monuments and practical information for visitors.

Photographs and illustrations were meant to capture the atmosphere of the Old Town and inspire tourists to visit it. Numerous nooks of the Old Town guarantee the authentic impressions: medieval alleys, stately palaces, cosy little coffeehouses on the corners and squares and finally kind and hospitable locals. We believe that our guidebook will contribute to your satisfaction and comfort and that you will be coming back to our "Pearl on the Danube River" as Bratislava is often referred to.

TABLE OF CONTENTS

SITUATION

The geographical position of Bratislava is very similar to that of the neighbouring Vienna or Budapest. These three Central European metropolises lie on the banks of the river Danube in places, where the great river leaves behind mountain ranges. Bratislava is only 65 kilometres from Vienna and only 50 from the Vienna's international airport of Schwechat. The distance between Bratislava and Budapest is 180 km,

and that between Bratislava and Prague is 330 km. The position of Bratislava is eccentric with regard to territory of the Slovakia. It is situated in its extreme south-western corner. A comparatively long section of the city border coincides with the frontier,

a rare phenomenon in comparison to other European capitals. Bratislava is one of the youngest European capitals. It was capital during the short existence of the Slovak State in the years 1939-1945. Later in 1993 it again became the capital of the independent Slovak Republic. The territory also referred to as Greater Bratislava has an area of 367.5 square kilometres with population 429,000 equalling to about eight per cent of Slovakia's total population.

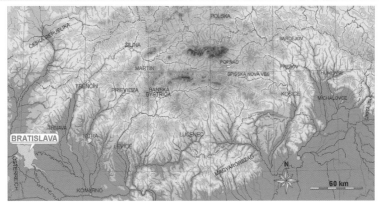

HISTORY

The history of creative presence of man in the territory of today's Bratislava goes back several thousand years. To know the first inhabitants of the town, we should go back as far as the Older Stone Age. The **Celts** brought a revolutionary change in the history of Bratislava. The Celtic tribes, which subdued a substantial part of the northern half of Europe, also settled in the territory of modern Bratislava. After a short Dacian episode, which took place short before the arrival of new era, another important period of Bratislava's history started, which can be called after the prevailing ethnicities the **German-Roman period.** As the Romans were not able to push the frontiers of the Empire up to the crests of the Carpathians, the territory of Bratislava became part of the turbulent contact zone separating often hostile Romans living south of the Danube and Germans ruling over the areas north of this great European river. For approximately four centuries the area im-

mediately neighbouring the Danube found itself on the border between two different worlds, which meant permanent political and economic instability. The part of modern Bratislava lying south of the Danube belonged to the Roman province of Pannonia administered by the Roman legions settled nearby in Carnuntum (today Bad Deutsch Altenburg in Austria). There were (within the territory administered now by the village of Rusovce) a Roman fort called **Gerulata** with a settlement bigger than usual and a market place.

The fall of the Roman Empire was followed by a cultural, economic and political vacuum. Several waves of migration passed over the territory of Bratislava during the **migration period** of the 4th to 6th centuries. The fact that the eastern frontier of the Frankish realm united by Charles the

1 Coronation of Maria Theresia at St. Martin's Minster
2 Villa rustica
3 Biatecs
4 Gerulata

Great stabilized amidst the territory inhabited mostly by the Slavs was especially important for Bratislava. Now it was in a boundary position. Charles´ descendants fighting between them for the crown of the successor state of the Western Roman Empire tried to conquer this territory. But they met with resistance from the Slav princes Mojmír and Pribina, who were not on particularly good terms with each other either. When the Mora-vian prince defeated his rival Pribina from Nitra and drove him out of the country, he built the stable foundations of the powerful though not long existing **Empire of Great Moravia**. A large portion of the populations of this new state formation, which reached its apex in the second half of the 9th century,

inhabited forts. Two of them were constructed in the territory of Bratislava. One was situated below the Devín castle rock, and the second occupied the castle hill of Bratislava.

The local fort was included into the settlement structure of the arising early feudal **Hungarian Kingdom**. Arpád's direct descendant **Stephen I** elected as the first King of Hungary in 1000 was even seated at the Bratislava castle for some time. The date of **December 2nd 1291** is not the date of birth of Pressburg. One should take it rather as the date of its school leaving certificate, which confirms the aptness of its inhabitants to become

1 and **2** the Devín Castle **3** Roman tombstone **4** Great Moravian basilica **5** Sts Constantine and Methodius **6** Sculpture from Gerulata

the free citizens of a royal borough. Important group of privileges provided for the economic development of the town. It concerned trade and the crafts. Another municipal privilege worth mentioning concerned the defence of the town. Only the royal boroughs were allowed to have municipal fortifications.

A special and above-standard relation originated between Pressburg

and the King Sigismund of Luxembourg who ascended to the throne in 1387 and reigned for fifty years, longer than any other Hungarian ruler. In 1430 Pressburg received another privilege, the right to strike coins in its own mint. The prestige of the town grew with the granting of a coat of arms in 1436. Ladislav's successor was Hunyady's son Matthias Corvinus. Traditional sympathy of the Hungarian sovereigns to Pressburg also continued during his thirty-year reign. Ceremonious confirmation of the privileged position of the town by **The Golden Bull of King Matthias** in

1464 and the addition of a new privilege, that of the sword, in 1468 manifested it. The name of King Matthias is connected with the penetration of humanistic ideas into Central Europe. The result of one such

inspiration was the opening of university, which followed the example of the oldest university at Bologna. Pressburg was chosen for the seat of this university and its name was **Universitas Istropolitana**.

1 Water tower below the Castle 2 Henry III below the Castle of Pressburg 3 The Act of Coat of Arms 4 The western town walls and St. Martin's Minster 5 The St. Clara church and monastery

DANVBIVS   FLV.

The defeat of combined Hungarian forces against Turks at the **battle of Mohács** in 1526 was disastrous for the country. The army of the Ottoman Sultan Süleyman II first deprived the country of its king and then of its freedom. But Pressburg paradoxically benefited from the situation. Ferdinand of Habsburg, confirmed by repeated coronation in Székesfehérvar a year after the Pressburg congress, compensated the town for its goodwill and promoted it to the capital of Hungary by the law

approved by the Hungarian Parliament in 1536. It was a temporary act. It would be in force only until the entire territory was won back from the Turks. The fall of Székesfehérvar meant that Hungary lost its traditional coronation town. This is how Pressburg won another privilege, the one of coronation of the Hungarian kings and their spouses. It was another, though temporary function to be kept until 1830 and used nineteen times. The period of greatest prosperity and expansion is connected with the

1 Pressburg in the 16th century
2 The column commemorating Turkish wars
3 Universitatis Istropolitana
4 Pressburg in the 18th century
5 and 6 Coronation feast next to St. Martin's Minster

forty-year rule of **Maria Theresia** on the Hungarian throne. Her indeed unusually positive relation to Pressburg may have originated on the day of her pompous coronation on June 25th 1741. After this she used every occasion to visit the beloved town. Thanks to the queen's favour the life of the town became more varied and refreshed by various attractive events and feasts. For the sake of comfort, many aristocrats decided to own residences or fashionable palaces in Pressburg.

Maria Theresia's wars with Prussia luckily did not affect Pressburg at all. A long period of peace similar to that in the 14th

century was repeated. All areas of human activity throve in such a favourable epoch: Trade, crafts, learn-

ing, education, arts, and spiritual life. The spirit of enlightenment and tolerance entered Pressburg. Number of its population increased more than three-

fold. The town sheltered 33 thousand inhabitants and it meant that Pressburg was the largest city in Hungary.

Pressburg was larger than Buda, Pest or Debrecen. The town was expanding and new suburbs were originating outside the inner walls. The municipal fortifications again became the principal obstacle to the further urbanistic development of Pressburg. It was obvious that the town had to be liberated from its restraining ring of the town walls.

Son of Maria Theresia, Emperor **Joseph II** was much less interested in Pressburg than his mother. The political position of Pressburg weakened during

1 Grassalkovich Palace **2** Maria Theresia **3** Coronation of Maria Theresia
4 Coronation ceremony in front of the eastern town walls

the reign of Joseph II although the city still had good conditions for economic growth.

The economic growth of Pressburg was slowed down by the Napoleonic Wars at the beginning of the 19th century. French troops came close to Pressburg twice. The first time was in 1805, when they easily took the town. A squad of thirty cavalrymen occupied the shuttle bridge over the Danube and opened the way to

three hundred cavalrymen and 9,000 infantry soldiers. Shortly after the Battle of Austerlitz (today Slavkov) took place. The peace treaty that entered history as the **Peace of Pressburg** confirmed Napoleon's famous victory. The documents were signed on December 26th 1805 in the Hall of Mirrors of the Primatial Palace. The treaty brought about great losses

of territory for the defeated kingdom.

The second half of the 19th century is characterized by the onset of the industrial revolution. The number of industrial plants working in the city jumped up to forty-one in the sixties. In 1869 there were 2,392 firms employing 5,293 workers. And before the end of the 19th century another 19 factories giving jobs to additional 1,700 people were founded. The development of industry was accompanied by that of modern transport. The introduction of

1 The Baroque interior of the Holy Trinity church **2** The principal altar in the Baroque Elizabethan church

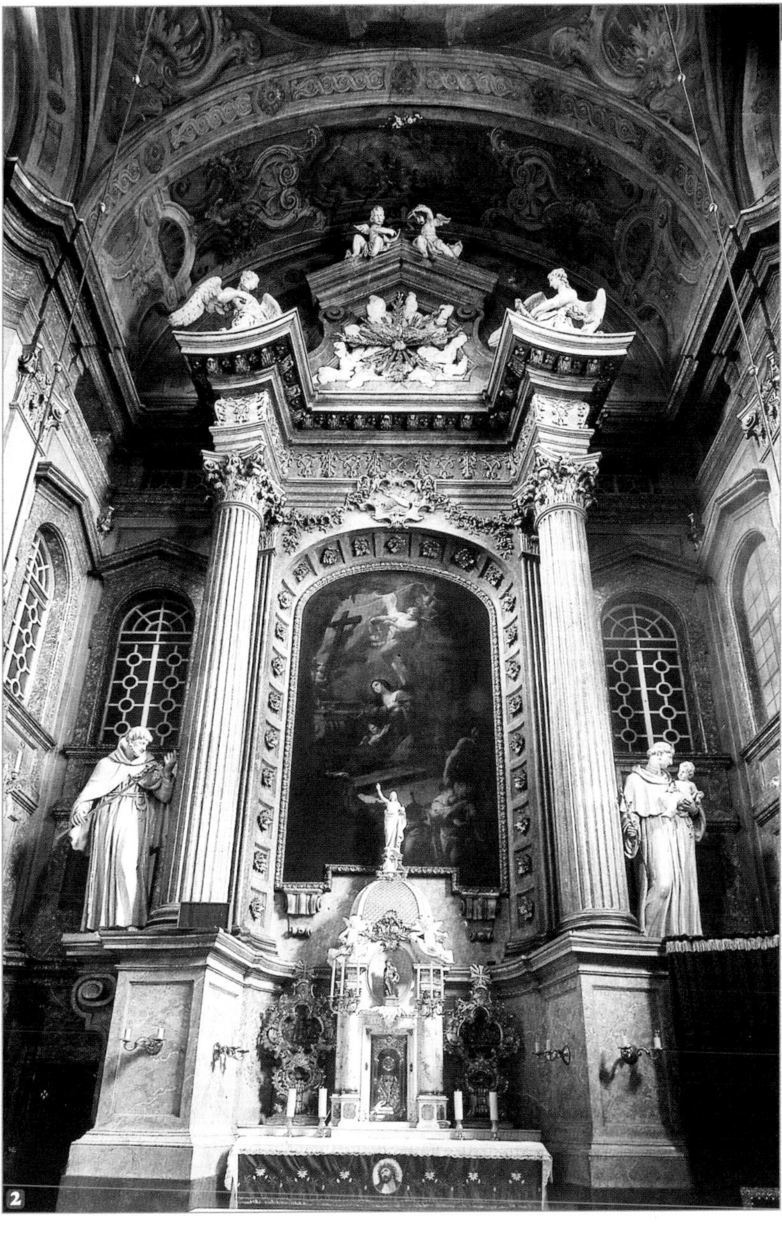

2

steam engine in river navigation in 1818 meant a revolutionary progress in the industry. Travelling to the right bank of the Danube by the Pressburg "propeller" was a favourite pastime of the citizens. The following year they even could walk to the Petržalka park via the first fixed bridge over the Danube, later called after the Emperor Franz Joseph. In 1840 the first train on

the horse railway left Pressburg for Svätý Jur. Pressburg did not lag too much behind the rest of the world in the sphere of steam engines. The first steam locomotive entered its railway station on August 30th 1848. The railway track of the trains going to Marcheg was later extended to Vienna, and this track is linked with the oldest railway bridge and tunnel in the former territory of Hungary. When in 1895 the first tram set out on a journey across the city, it meant the beginnings of the modern municipal transport. Trolley buses were introduced in 1911.

Pressburg was spared the direct impact of the First World War. The population suffered from the war only indirectly. Nevertheless, the war lasted longer for the citizens of Pressburg. When the arms stopped firing on all

1 Coronation feast
2 The hills of Bratislava in the 19th century
3 Statue of St. Martin
4 Františkánske nám. square in the 19th century

fronts, the battle for Pressburg only began. When the Czechoslovak Republic was declared on the ruins of the Monarchy on October 28th 1918 and two days later was confirmed in Martin by the Slovak National Council, the destiny of Pressburg was unclear.

On February 2nd 1919 the Slovak Government led by Vavro Šrobár moved from Žilina to Pressburg, which became the capital of Slovakia. Pressburg lasted only for another month, because on March

6th 1919 its **name was changed to Bratislava**. The first years of Bratislava in interwar Czechoslovakia were the ones of establishment of numerous national institutions, such as the Slovak National Theatre, Comenius University, etc. The population increased from 83,000 in 1919 to 124,000 in 1938. Bratislava remained a city of three nationalities also after the disintegration of Monarchy, only in different ratios. The share of Slovaks (and Czechs) increased from 33 % in 1919 to 59 % in 1938 (Czechs were represented by 17 %). The share of Germans dropped in the same period from 36 to 22 %, and in case of Hungarians it was from 29 to 13 %.

When on March 14th 1939 the independent Slovak State was declared, **Bratislava became its capital**. President Jozef Tiso had his seat in Grassalkowich's Palace. The state created under the pressure of the Nazi Germany did not last long. It practically disappeared in April 1945 with the entry of the Red Army ac-

1 The Classicist Primatial Palace
2 The embankment of the Danube in the 19th century
3 The embankment of the Danube today

in search of jobs and possibility to obtain flats. The post-war city was experiencing an unusual boom. But it has to be said that the development

companied by the Romanian troops. Bratislava was also expanding during the Second World War. In four decades the population of the city

was extensive. Mass construction of housing estates started. Flats were built but the basic amenities lagged behind. In 1978 construction of flats continued on the right bank of the Danube, in

quadrupled. The extreme population increase was attributed to in-migration from the whole of Slovakia. People were coming

1 Station of horse railway
2 The tram from Pressburg to Vienna
3 The Red Bridge 4 Bratislava in 20th century 5 Pontoon bridge over the Danube
6 Nový most bridge
7 The fount of Družba on the Námestie slobody square 8 Blue Church
9 Presidential Palace

Petržalka. Petržalka with its 120,000 inhabitants became in ten years the biggest housing estate in Czechoslovakia. This extensive growth stopped after the November 1989 revolution and the population stabilized for the whole following decade at about 450,000. **Bratislava became again the capital of the independent Slovak Republic** after the division of the Czech and Slovak Federal Republic on January 1st 1993.

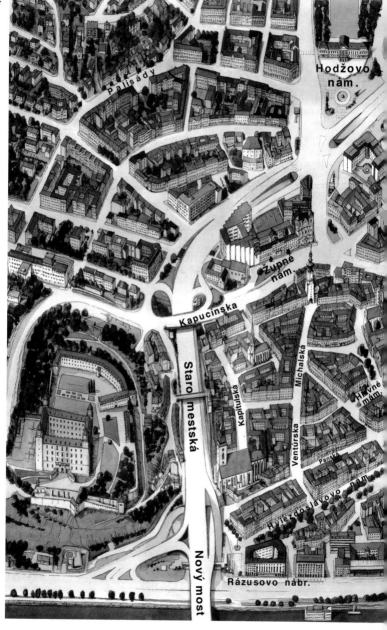

Palisády

Hodžovo nám.

Župné nám.

Kapucínska

Staromestská

Kapitulská

Michalská

Hlavné nám.

Venturska

Panská

Hviezdoslavovo nám.

Nový most

Rázusovo nábr.

Kollárovo nám.

Obchodná

Špitálska

Nám. SNP

Dunajská

Laurinská

Štúrova

Vajanského nábr.

OLD TOWN

The centre of Bratislava is also referred to as the Staré Mesto or the Old Town (134 m above sea level, population 44,800). It became the district of Bratislava I in 1996 and its area 9.6 square kilometres makes it the smallest one of Slovakia. It is simultaneously the most densely populated district (4,790 inhabitants per square km). The Old Town includes the historic core of the city and adjacent quarters, originally medieval suburbs. The eastern part of the Old Town is flat and covered by dense urban fabric. The western part lies on the hills with greater part of urban greenery

1 Old Town seen from the tower of the old Town Hall
2 and **3** Old Town seen from the Castle

compared to the rest of the city. The southern limit of the Old Town coincides with the channel of the Danube.

Michalská and Ventúrska streets

You should start at the Hviezdoslavovo námestie square with a wonderful view of the slender silhouette of Michalská veža tower with its typical onion-shaped roof. The

1 Michalská street at the beginning of the 20th century
2 Michalská street today 3 Bridge of St. Michael

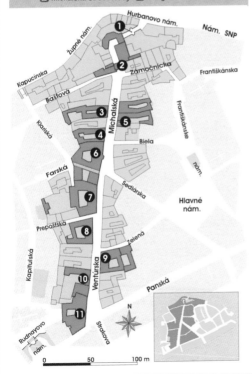

beginning of Michalská street runs along the old stone **bridge of St. Michael**** ❶ over the former water moat. It was built in the first half of the 18th century and replaced the original wooden drawbridge. On the left side of the bridge the passers-by get a nice view of the rest of the former town moat. Left from the Michalská veža tower the parts of the double town walls have been preserved. The upper section of Michalská ulica passes through the preserved remains of barbican, which protected the entry into the inner town from the 15th century. The curve of the street was intentional as it prevented the direct artillery attacks on the actual **Michalská brána** gate.

Before passing under the Michalská brána gate do not forget to look at the narrow house on its right side. It is **house** with the narrowest facade in the city (1.6 m), which documents the skills of Bratislava's medieval builders when they had to come on terms with the limited space inside the town walls. The width of this extremely narrow house corresponds to that of the moat and its peripheral walls coincide with those of fortifications.

The **Michalská veža***** ❷ tower constitutes one of the symbols of the city. It is the only one preserved out of four providing for the entry into the fortified medieval town. It provided for the passage into the town from the north, coming from the Záhorie or Moravian regions. In the night it was closed. Its name derives from the village that existed in early Middle Ages beyond the gate and around the long before demolished church of St. Michael. The tower has seven floors now. One can identify several architectural styles from Gothic to Baroque. The lowest part is the passage with a brick cross vault and five floors of a massive four-sided tower. The part from the second floor down to the ground is the oldest. It originated as a Gothic fortified gate sometime in the first half of the 14th century. The rest of the prism with another three floors was added in the first

third of the 16th century when Turkish attacks were expected and the city was more thoroughly fortified.

Under the tower is the **zero kilometre,** from which the distances of the individual world

settlements are calculated. Ascent to the gallery of Michalská tower is worthwhile as you can also see an **exhibition of historic arms** from the Town Museum deposited in the tower. The

panoramic view from the top of the tower is superb.

The view of the near Zámočnícka and Baštová streets deserves special attention. These two streets originated as narrow castle lanes in the immediate vicinity of the town walls. On the left there is Zámočnícka ulica street. Its name (Smith's street) reveals that there were workshops of craftsmen here in the past. The fire of 1590 destroyed its original Gothic buildings. On the right of the tower is Baštová ulica street. Its name derives from the bastions, which used to be part of the defensive system north of the street. The headsman used to live in this street and that is why the name of the street before 1879 was Katova or Headsman's street. Standing at the Michalská

tower one gets a view of the whole of **Michalská ulica** street, which is one of the oldest in the city. Its lower part existed as early as the Romanesque period of Pressburg. Later it was widened by the addition of more houses along the road used by merchants on their way from the north to Bratislava's ford over the Danube. The builders of the inner town walls set its present length sometime in the 14th century. The modern urban fabric of Michalská street is varied in styles with prevailing preserved or restored Renaissance houses.

Let us stop first at **Segner's curia**** ❸ (house No. 7) in the western row of houses, which attracts attention with its two two-storied oriels. It is also the house where Johann Andreas Segner (1704-

❶ Barbican and the Most Holy Trinity church
❷ Baštová street ❸ Underpass below the St. Michael tower ❹ Underpass below the barbican

remote past breathes from the white walls with tender arches. The chapel is one of the oldest surviving buildings of Bratislava.

The most magnificent building of Michalská street is at its lower end. It is the **Palace of the Hungarian Royal Court Chamber** ❻**, today the University Library. In its central hall the lower council of the Hungarian Parliament formed by the county deputies, free royal boroughs, and chapters, had its sessions in the years 1802-1848. The building was adapted to the needs of the University Library, its present purpose, in the years 1951-1953.

The Ventúrska ulica street, continuing Michalská, bears the name of the family Ventura from Italy. Ventúrska street is connected

1777), a scientist of European rank was born. **Jeszenák Palace* ❹** (house No. 3), built in 1730 as a city palace, is the second oldest of Bratislava. Only Esterházy's palace in Kapitulská street is older. The royal counsellor Pavol Jeszenák built it in the 17th century.

A comparatively modest building with simple Neo Classical facade standing on the eastern side of Michalská street hides a pleasant surprise: the wonderful Gothic interior of the **Chapel of St. Catharine** ❺**. The charm of the with Michalská by a short tapered section caused by close proximity of the facing houses. One of the buildings forming this bottle neck is the **Palace of Leopold de Pauli** ❼ (house No. 13). It was built in the years 1777-1776 for the main administrator of the royal property on the former royal plot. Gothic houses probably occupied the site before. The chamber architect F. K. Römisch, who probably followed the design of Hillebrandt, built it. De Pauli's city palace is a nice sample of the new trend in the architecture of Pressburg's city palaces applied in the last quarter of the 18th century. This palace has got all that is absent in other palaces. In its interior there is a garden with a graceful Rococo **music pavilion**. Some sources assert that in 1820 **Franz Liszt** gave a concert there. The corner of Ventúrska and Prepoštská streets is occupied by **Zichy**

Palace ❽ (house No. 11) with its smart and strictly Neo Classical facade. Its builder was F. Feline. It was built on the site of three older medieval houses as a four-wing building with inner gallery-rimmed courtyard. Count Franz Zichy had it built in 1775. The palace was restored for the purpose of ceremonies and feasts in the 1980's. **Pálffy Palace** ❾ (house No. 10) which was reconstructed in 1747 stands on the corner of Ventúrska and Zelená streets. The tablet on the facade of Pálffy's palace facing Ventúrska street announces that it was presumably the venue of the concert of the then six year old child known by the whole world as **Wolfgang Amadeus Mozart** (1756-1791). In two venerable looking houses opposite Pálffy's palace the history of university education in Pressburg started more than 500 years ago. It includes the thirty-year lasting activity of the first humanistic university in Hungary known as the **Universitas Istropolitana** ❿.

The Ventúrska street slightly widens in its lower part. The narrow triangle is very probably the remnant of an old market place from the beginnings of the medieval settlement below the castle. Its western part is occupied by **Erdődy's palace**** ⓫ (house No. 1). The former private seat of the state judge Count Juraj Erdödy is the last palace built in Pressburg from

the second generation of the city palaces. The local architect Matej Walch finished it in 1770. Originally there were two floors and in the first half of the 20th century a third floor was built on top of them.

❶ University library ❷ The lower part of Ventúrska street ❸ and ❹ St. Martin's Minster seen from the Castle

St. Martin's Minster and Kapitulská street

The pride of every Christian city is its parish church. This is undoubtedly the case with **St. Martin's Minster****** **❶**, Bratislava's biggest, oldest and most spectacular church. St. Martin's Minster

was a **coronation church** in the years 1563-1830. The first ruler to be crowned here was Maximillian II. The coronation ceremony took place on September 8th 1563. It was followed by eighteen other coronations including that of Maria Theresia on June 25th 1741. The last king who received St. Stephen's royal crown below the lead statue of St. Martin was Ferdinand V on September 28th 1830. An incomplete list of eleven kings and eight royal spouses crowned in Pressburg's Minster is on the board placed on the inside northern wall. Reconstruction in the Baroque taste first concentrated on the interior and later on the construction of the fourth chapel. In the years 1732-1734 the ground plan of the church was widened by the **chapel of St. John the Almsgiver** one of the most valuable artistic monuments of Bratislava. The Baroque chapel was probably built according to the George Raphael Donner's

design (1693-1741). The recognized artist Georg Rafael Donner was entrusted with more works in the interior of the church. The new bulky Baroque altar with Donner's monumental **group of statues of St. Martin** replaced the removed Gothic one. This wonderful sculpture made in 1744 from lead represents a Roman soldier from Transdanubian Pannonia, who cuts his cape in two in a mighty movement of sabre to give half of it to a beggar suffering from cold.

The Baroque **tower** was is a gilded 2x2 m cushion bearing the copy of the Hungarian royal crown. The imitation is one metre tall and weighs 300 kilograms. The visitors of Bratislava Minster's monumental interior of 70x23 metres

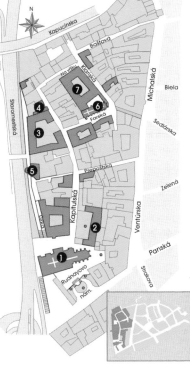

destroyed by fire caused by lightning in 1833. It was only three years after the last coronation was held in the Minster. Reconstruction was entrusted to an important Pressburg Classicist architect Ignác Feigler senior. He chose the fashionable romanticizing style. The tower was given the Neo Gothic face, which has survived until today. The tower of the Minster is 85 metres tall. At its top

can admire there many remarkable works of art, and others are deposited in the parts of the church closed to the public.

The street leading northward from presbytery of the Minster is called Kapitulská. Its length was determined by the town fortifications at its northern end. This is one of the oldest streets of the town and the Church dignitaries, who were

moved from the castle to the settlement below the castle by the beginning of the 13th century, created it. The houses of provost, canons and priests formed the street. It used to be the main street of the Romanesque Pressburg.

1 Gothic windows
2 The bust of Franz Liszt
3 Coronation of Carolina Augusta

It ran further to Zámocká ulica and the Castle. Expansion of the town in the 14th century pushed the street to the western edge of the town.

In the right corner, at the end of the eastern row of houses of Kapitulská ulica street stands a big building with a comparatively large forecourt. It originated in 1632 by reconstruction of an older house as ordered by the then provost Juraj Draškovič. The provost used it and this is the reason why it is called the **Provost's Palace** ❷**. The present Provost's Palace though, is a two-storied Renaissance building with short lateral wings, which close the mentioned forecourt or rather a garden. The Provost's Palace is today the seminary for priests.

The **Esterházy Palace* ❸** (house Nos. 6-10) is the only secular building on Kapitulská street. It is one of the oldest palaces in the city, as it was built almost a century before the city was seized by building frenzy in time of Maria Theresia, which gave origin to plenty of wonderful Baroque, Roco-

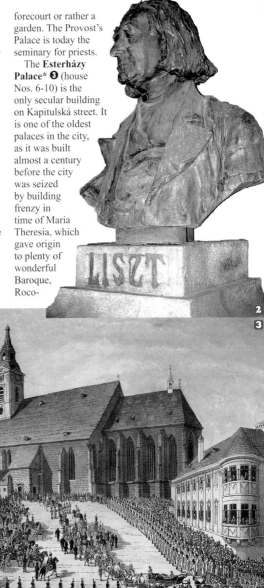

co, and Neo Classical palaces. It was built in the mid-17th century and restored in the Baroque style in the following century. The Listh family owned the original house.

street called the **Small Provost's House*** ❹ will certainly attract the visitor's attention. It consists of two Gothic houses from the 15th century. Behind the eastern

Later Count Esterházy bought it. The governor Albert, son-in-law of Queen Maria Theresia also lived in the house for some time.

The venerable looking Gothic house No. 4 in the northern part of Kapitulská

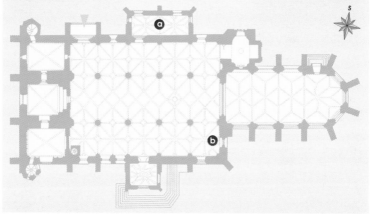

Ground plan of St. Martin's Minster
❹ Chapel of St. John Almsgiver ❺ Statue of St. Martin

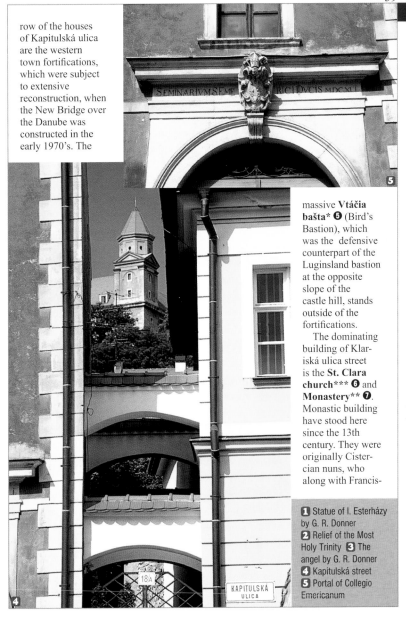

row of the houses of Kapitulská ulica are the western town fortifications, which were subject to extensive reconstruction, when the New Bridge over the Danube was constructed in the early 1970's. The

massive **Vtáčia bašta*** ❺ (Bird's Bastion), which was the defensive counterpart of the Luginsland bastion at the opposite slope of the castle hill, stands outside of the fortifications.

The dominating building of Klariská ulica street is the **St. Clara church***** ❻ and **Monastery**** ❼. Monastic building have stood here since the 13th century. They were originally Cistercian nuns, who along with Francis-

❶ Statue of I. Esterházy by G. R. Donner
❷ Relief of the Most Holy Trinity ❸ The angel by G. R. Donner
❹ Kapitulská street
❺ Portal of Collegio Emericanum

can monks, were the first to come to Pressburg. By the end of the 13th century the Gothic nave of the church was started and it was finished in 1375. The vault of the church had to be restored again after fire in 1515. Presbytery was added to the nave and both are vaulted with ribbed cross vaults. In the early 15th century a five-sided Gothic tower lavishly adorned by pinnacles, gargoyles and little statues in what is called the Beautiful Style was added on the side of Farská ulica street. Today there are true copies of four statues on the tower. The original statues are kept inside the church. This Bratislava's landmark is impressive not only for its beauty, but also for its bold architectural solution. The builder decided for an unconventional approach when he did not build the tower on the foundations buried in earth. He rather built it on the lateral wall

1 Kapitulská street 2 Tower of St. Clara church
3 Portal of St. Clara church 4 Statue of St. Elisabeth of Hungary

of the church nave.

The original Gothic monastery of St. Clara became dilapidated, when the nuns left Pressburg fleeing from the Turks in 1526. The order moved to Trnava. Later they came back only to face ownership problems with the city and the consequences of another fire. Finally it was Archbishop Peter Pázmány who decided for a deep change of architecture of the monastery. He sup-ported all Catholic institutions within the framework of the Re-Catholicizing program of the Church and also helped to the nuns of St. Clara's order. The new monastery was built on the foundations of the old. The former monastery was reconstructed in the years 1957-1961 and it became the seat of the Slovak Pedagogic Library. The monastery now shelters the Office of the European Council.

Panská and Laurinská streets

Panská and Laurinská streets form together the longest street line in the historical centre of Bratislava with total length of 700 m. In the past they bore the common name of Dlhá or Long street. The more easterly-situated Laurinská is busier with more shops and less luxurious houses. Panská (or Lordly) street is what its name suggests, as there are many city palaces, which used to belong to the nobility and rich burgers.

Panská ulica street starts at the former Vydrická brána gate and ends at the crossroads with Rybárska brána. The Neo Classical

Csáky Palace** ❶
stands at the point, where Panská ulica street opens to the rectangular area of Rudnay's square. The domestic builder Matúš Walch built it for Count

Juraj Csáky in 1775. The **Keglevich Palace** ❷** stands on the corner of Panská and Strakova street. Side by side the proud Erdödy Palace it looks like a country mansion of some yeoman from the north of Slovakia. The short facade of the single floor house compensated by the tall red roof typical of old village mansions causes this rustic impression. The Baroque palace originated by rebuilding an older burgher house.

The **Pálffy Palace*** ❸** at Panská No. 19-21 revealed some pleasant surprises to the historians and archaeologists in recent years. The oldest written documents relating to this palace on today's Panská

street are from 1415 to 1516. The Pálffy family bought the house in 1715. Count Pálffy was later nominated palatine and state judge. He paid thirty thousand guldens for the house. In

the first half of the 19th century the Pálffys unified the original building in the Neo Classical style with the facade preserved up to now. In 1885 the rear parts of the palace were pulled down and a new palace was built facing the Promenade. Extensive reconstruction of the interior of the palace carried out in the 1980's adjusted the palace for the purpose of **Art Gallery of the city of Bratislava**.

A defensive tower occupied the site of house No. 17, now used by the **British Council* ❹**, in the 13th century. The Gothic house from the 15th century belonged to palatine Rozgoň, the protagonist of the civil war between the Castle and the town. The owners of the

house alternated until the Pauline monks from Marianka bought it. The Paulines wore typical white gowns and that is why the house was called The House of the White Monks. In the second half of the 17th century the Paulines changed the back part of the house into a chapel of the Most Holy Trinity. The later owners of the house pulled down the chapel of which only the Early Baroque portal with the year 1671 carved in it has survived.

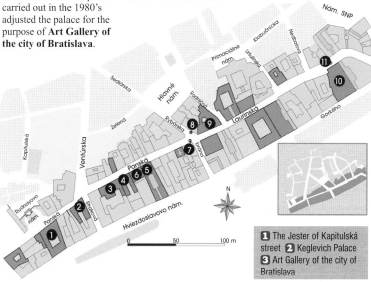

❶ The Jester of Kapitulská street **❷** Keglevich Palace **❸** Art Gallery of the city of Bratislava

Let us go back to the southern part of Panská. In its middle there are two palaces. It is good they are standing side by side because we can compare the heavy, majestic Baroque building with the light and graceful Rococo house. **Esterházy Palace**** ❺ (No. 13) on the left was built in 1743 for Count Ján Esterházy, a member of one of the richest noble families in Hungary. The palace was one of the most luxurious in the city, though its exterior does not confirm it. The Rococo **Balassa Palace**** ❻ standing on the right (No. 15) is quite different from its neighbour. The three-storied house is lower, less massive and the ornamentation of the facade is considerably finer and more elaborate. The Rococo sculptured ornamentation of the facade is full of symbols and allegories of the Classical deities.

The crossroads of Rybárska brána, Panská and Laurinská street is certainly the liveliest spot of the city. People like to stop here to listen to the street musicians and the tourists love to have a snap made with **Čumil**** ❼ in background. Rybárska brána street is a short street in the historic centre of Bratislava and part of the already mentioned Corso. It is a pedestrian zone between Hlavné námestie and Hviezdoslavovo námestie squares.

Next to house No. 1 stands a life-size statue with a top hat in his hand and a welcoming gesture. In contrast to the statue of Čumil this one painted in gleaming silver paint represents a real person, a native of Bratislava nicknamed **Schöner Náci** (Fair Náci)** ❽. His real name was Ignác Lamar, and he was born on August 12th, 1897 into the family of a shoemaker in Petržalka. Schöner Náci frequented Bratislava's pubs and coffee houses and became an inseparable part of the city's folklore.

Laurinská ulica street is the prolongation of Panská. It starts at Rybárska brána and ends in Štúrova. The first (**No. 1**)* ❾ in the northern row of houses on Laurinská is a four-storied house with a Neo Classical facade. It was built after design of Ignác Feigler Senior in 1846. First of all it was the seat of the First Pressburg Saving Bank founded in 1842 as the oldest bank institution in the city. Opposite the First Pressburg Savings Bank is a modern corner building, the House of the Slovak Writers. There is a bookshop in its ground floor. On the corner of Laurinská and Radničná the Neo Classical house

① Carnival on Laurinská street ② Schöner Náci
③ Laurinská street ④ Čumil (The Gazer)

of Baron Walterskirchen (No. 3) was built in the 19th century. At the eastern end of Laurinská street stands the theatre building of **Divadlo P. O. Hviezdoslava*** ❿. A copy of bars hangs across the street and above the heads of passers by just to remind us that it is the place where **Laurin-ská brána*** ⓫ gate used to stand. The first reference to the gate is from 1412, and it even quotes the salary of the gatekeeper. Laurinská brána was pulled down in 1778.

The Hlavné námestie square

Out of the three central areas in the historic centre of Bratislava the **Hlavné námestie** square (The Main Square) with its squarish ground plan is the most impressive one. Through the history it was the stage and witness to

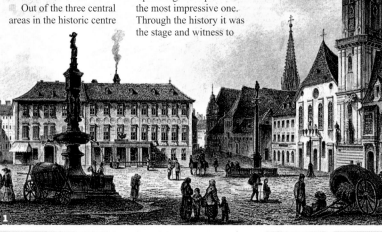

1 and **2** Hlavné námestie square in the 19th century and today
3 Old Town Hall **4** Maximillian's fount

practically every important event, which took place in the town. It used to be the main market place, stage for the Passion plays, gatherings, and the place, where the rulers were greeted and welcomed, but also where executions or public punishments were carried out. The splendid coronation trail headed by a new King of Hungary always attracted the crowds to Hlavné námestie. The affection of Bratislava's citizens toward their square

survived. They still like to go to traditional Christmas fair, performances of musical bands, tower concerts of trumpeters or simply to relax next to the Renaissance fountain or under the sunshades of cafés.

People often meet next to **Maximilian's fountain**** ❶ in the western part of the square perhaps the same as Londoners meet at Piccadilly Circus under Cupid's statue. The square lacked a public

water source until the
second half of the 16th
century. Only in 1572 the
financial contribution of
King Maximilian II made
it possible to finish the
fountain, which now bears
his name and portrait.

Every building at Hlavné
námestie deserves atten-
tion. The most important
of them is the **Stará
radnica****** ❷ or the
Old Town Hall. Pressburg
was the first town in the
Upper Hungary to acquire
the building of Town Hall
of its own. The municipal
council had its sessions in
Jacob's house even before
the town bought it. The rebuilt Pressburg Town Hall
on Hlavné námestie was
fully used only after 1434.

A new passage opening the
entry into the Town Hall
from the square was made
before 1442. This remark-
able architectural element

has been preserved in its
full beauty up till now.

The Town Hall of Press-
burg entered the 16th
century in a new Late

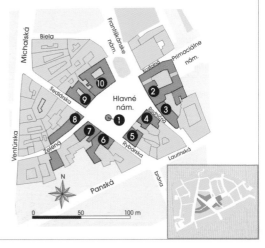

Gothic shell and became the dominant building of the square and an important part of the city's silhouette. In the second half of the 16th century the tower of the Town Hall was slightly adjusted to the principles of the Renaissance style. Six identical **Renaissance windows** were put into the facade facing the square; Unger's house had another two from 1581. **Renaissance arcades** on pillars, preserved up to now, and

made by the stonemason Bartolomej from Wolfstahl were added in 1581. But the most beautiful thing that happened to the Town Hall came at the end of the 17th century when B. C. Orsati made the lavish stucco ornamentation of

the rooms: rims of the vaults and frames in which the painter J. J. Drentwett from Augsburg placed beautiful **wall paintings**. He followed in style the Italian and Flemish patterns of the 17th century. The painting placed in the middle of the vault represents the theme of the Last Judgement. The project was completed in 1912 and it involved construction of the eastern and southern wings of the Town Hall.

1 The yard of the Old Town Hall **2** Old Town Hall **3** The detail of the ceiling in the underpass of the Old Town Hall **4** Radničná street **5** interior of the Old Town Hall

50

All later interventions were mere repairs and reconstruction of some hidden valuable architectural details. While restoring the facade the **cannon ball** stuck in the facade, which commemorates the attacks of Napoleon's army in 1809 was also preserved. There is also a **board with a line** marking the water level of the Danube at the time of the disastrous floods on February 5th 1850.

The **Apponyi Palace**** ❸ next to Unger's house is out of the Hlavné námestie square in a short Radničná ulica street. It was built in the years 1761-1762 for count Juraj Apponyi, a member of a rich Hungarian noble family from Oponice near Topoľčany. At present the Apponyi Palace shelters the **Viticultural Museum** and regional library. The collections displayed on the ground floor and basement of the palace document the rich history of wine growing in

the traditional viticultural region of the Little Carpathians. An original press used in wine production is placed in the courtyard.

The **house*** ❹ (No. 2) standing opposite the

Apponyi Palace with its main entrance from the Hlavné námestie square is one of the oldest in the city. Due to remarkable discoveries of very old architectural elements from the last third of the 13th century the citizens of Pressburg know it as a house with a tower. Extensive renovation of the building in the 1980's of the 20th century led to discovery of the remains of an original burgher house with tower which was, like the predecessor of the Old Town Hall, made for living. The last of the trio of houses at the southern part of Hlavné námestie is the **Jeszenák Palace*** ❺. The Baroque building on the corner of Hlavné námestie and Rybárska brána was built in the 18th century at the site of an older house. The stone cartouche on corner bears the coat of arms of the original owner of the palace, Baron Ján Jeszenák. Recently the stylish and in the

❶ Emperor Maximillian II ❷ Façade of Unger's house
❸ Chess automate ❹ The yard of the Old Town Hall

past very popular **café** and sweet shop **Café Mayer** returned to the ground floor of the palace. The western row of houses at Hlavné námestie is the youngest one. **House No. 5** is especially interesting. It was built in 1906 on the site of an older medieval house of the Auer family from the 15th century. Queen Mary, the widow of King Louis II lived in it for some time. Today it is the seat of bank, but it has also the **café U Rolanda* ❻** on its ground floor. The interior of the café was refreshed by a true imitation of Kempelen's chess automate. The **Palugyay Palace* ❼** (No. 6)

standing on the corner of Hlavné námestie and Zelená Ulica street acquired its Neo Baroque appearance in 1880. The style is based on the traditions of the French Baroque. The opposite corner of Zelená ulica street is occupied by the **Zelený dom** ❽** or the Green House (Sedlárska street No. 12). The name derives from the green painted facade and in its ground floor was a popular tavern and restaurant. The front

wing of the Zelený dom overlooks the Sedlárska ulica street. Today this street is the favourite route

of walks. In the sixties of the 20th century the avantgarde theatre of *Divadlo na korze* (now the building of the Hungarian embassy) attracted the young audience, while today it is rather the Irish pub **The Dubliner**.

Let us go back to the Hlavné námestie square along the western wing of the **Kutscherfeld Palace** ❾** turned to Sedlárska street. The windows of the palace (No. 7) overlook Maximilian's fountain. The corner two-storied palace is one of the most beautiful Rococo buildings in the city. It was built in 1762 on the site of several medieval plots. Today the Kutscherfeld Palace houses the French embassy and the French Institute. The presence of the French on Hlavné námestie square is suggested also by the bronze statue of an Frenchman, the man in uniform wearing a typical three-horn Napoleon hat. The soldier looking like

52

shots. When in 1723 the **Palace of royal governing council**** ❿ was established, Pressburg was chosen as its seat. It was placed in the house in the north-eastern corner of Hlavné námestie. The city obtained this top office which represented the ruler in Hungary seated in Vienna. It was not entitled to take final decisions as it had to have them approved by the ruler represented by the Hungarian Office in Vienna. In 1762 the office also bought the neighbouring house. The two buildings were connected and rebuilt as the palace of the royal governing council. The eastern facade of the palace faces Františkánske námestie square and its southern side overlooks the Hlavné námestie square. The two-storied building with interior courtyard was reconstructed in Rococo style. The carriages entered the yard from the Hlavné námestie square and left it by the exit to Františkánske námestie square or vice versa. There is again a top governmental body seated in the palace now: the **Office of the Government of the Slovak Republic**.

Napoleon himself leans on a bench, a favourite spot of the tourists making snap-

1 Historic festival **2** Hlavné námestie square **3** Franciscan monastery

The Františkánske námestie square

The Františkánske námestie square is a kind of counterpart to busy Hlavné námestie or the Main square. It offers a much quieter, almost chamber ambience amidst antique historic houses. Františkánske námestie originated some time in the 13th century, hence it is one of the oldest in the town. Its present name is linked to the presence of the church and monastery of the Franciscan order.

The **Mirbach Palace***** ❶ is the architectural gem of the upper part of the Františkánske námestie square. It is rightly admired along with the Primatial Palace as one of the most beautiful sights offered by Bratislava. This Rococo building was built by Matej Hörlligl in years 1768-1770 on the site of the former Weitenhof house (Wide Yard House). It was a city property bought from the Franciscans. The Mirbach Palace was presumably built for a rich brewer of Pressburg, M. Spech. However, he sold it immediately after it was finished to Imrich Csáky. The owners of the palace alternated until Count Emil Mirbach bought it and eventually donated to the city in his last will, with the condition that it would become an art gallery. The city fulfilled the principal condition of the testament. The **Art Gallery of Bratislava** is located in the palace and offers valuable occasional fine art expositions along with standing collections of the Baroque artists whose work or life was connected with Bratislava.

Opposite to the Mirbach Palace is the Franciscan church. Let us stop first at the neighbouring building of

54

the **monastery**** ❷, the history of which is closely connected with this

❶ The detail of the portal of Mirbach Palace ❷ The Art Gallery of Bratislava ❸ Mirbach Palace ❹ Presbytery of Franciscan church ❺ Promotion to the Knight of the Golden Spur

church. It used to belong to the monks, who settled in the town in 1238. Inside the monastic complex the original arcade stations of cross-corridor built around the squarish cloister have survived. The present facade of the main monastic building facing Františkánske námestie

dates from the latter half of the 19th century.

The **Franciscan church***** ❸ consecrated to the Annunciation of the Virgin Mary is very old. It is the oldest preserved sacral building in Bratislava. Unconfirmed sources have that it was built by the King of

Hungary Ladislav IV Kumánsky in honour of the victory over the King Přemysl Otakar II of Bohemia in the famous battle on the Marchfeld in 1278. It was built in Gothic taste as a simple single-naved church. The earthquake of 1590 caused the fall of the Gothic cross vault. It was replaced by a new Renaissance vault. The original Gothic presbytery and the lateral walls of the nave were preserved

and today are the oldest part of the church. One of traditional ceremonies of the Pressburg coronations took place in the Franciscan church. It was the promotion of selected aristocrats to the Knights of the Golden Spur.

The **Jesuit Church**** ➍ in the lower part of the square was not always owned by the Jesuits. The German Evangelicals of

Sightseeing of the square ends under the **pillar of the Virgin Mary the Victorious** ❺** which is the oldest of the kind in the Kingdom of Hungary. It belongs to the group of pillars built by the Habsburg's all over the country in honour of their military successes. The one of Františkánske námestie stands here since 1675.

Pressburg built the church following the royal consent in 1636. The re-Catholicizing pressure became stronger during the reign of King Leopold I and Archbishop Szelepcsényi took away the temple of the Evangelicals. The German church was given to the Jesuits who dedicated it to the Most Holy Saviour. The new administrators of the church started its reconstruction. The facade remained almost intact, except for the original Renaissance portal. Jesuits installed a lavishly ornamented and multi-coloured symbol of their order on it. The main altar from the 19th century bears the picture of Christ on the Mountain of Tábor by S. Majsch.

❶ Chapel of the Franciscan church ❷ The window of burgher house on the Františkánske námestie square ❸ Entrance of the Jesuit church ❹ St. George fount

The Primaciálne námestie square

Comparatively young buildings surround the **Primaciálne námestie** square (The Primatial square), with the oldest house counting not more than four hundred years. But that does not mean that the square is young. The **Primatial Palace**** ❶**, which with his bulky building occupies the whole southern side of the Primatial square, is considered the most beautiful in Bratislava. It was built in the years 1778-1781 on the site of an older Archbishop's palace. The

front wing overlooking the Primatial square is strictly Neo Classical.

One enters the Primatial Palace through a three-axial vestibule where

a wide flight of stairs leads to the main halls on the first floor or Piano nobile. It overlooks the square and is directly connected with the main representative hall of the palace in its eastern wing. The huge hall looks even bigger because of the numerous mirrors on its walls. It is called the **Zrkadlová sieň** or the Hall of Mirrors. The role of the mirrors was to make the hall look bigger but above all to improve the lighting. The 1805 Christmas season was a time celebrated by the French as one of their historic moments. After

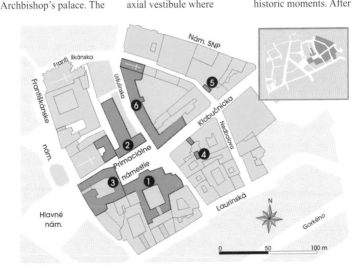

the battle at Austerlitz representatives of the countries which took part in it met in the Primatial Palace. The victorious Napoleon Bonaparte was represented by his Minister of Foreign Affairs Maurice Talleyrand and Prince John of Liechtenstein represented the defeated Emperor Francis. The treaty, later called the **Peace of Pressburg** was signed on December 26th 1805 in the Hall of Mirrors. Austria lost the territories of Tyrol, Istria, Dalmatia, and Venice and its access to the sea. France gained self-assurance and greed.

The city bought the palace in 1903 with

the intention to expand the Town Hall. During reconstruction of the palace some folded pieces of cloth were found. When they were spread on the floor of the corridor, the astounded custodian of the Municipal Museum August Heimar found out that it was a series of precious tapestries now known as the **Bratislava tapestries**. The Archbishop as owner of the palace gave up the precious find in favour of the city with the particular that they would be displayed in public. But first they had to be restored in the artistic workshops of Belmonte in Hungarian town of Gödöllő. The German expert and connoisseur of tapestries W. Zisch from Berlin estimated that the tapestries of Bratislava were made at the royal weaving workshop at Mortlake near London. The trade mark woven into the edge used by this particular

1 Primatial Palace today 2 Primatial Palace in the 19th century 3 Bratislava tapestry
4 Primaciálne námestie square seen from the tower of the Old Town Hall

workshop in the years 1616-1688 is the proof. The series of tapestries was made after the cartoons painted by Francis Cleyn from Rostock. Tapestries were woven on wool and silk and the style of this true work of art is called mannerism.

In the vestibule there is also a passage to the inner square courtyard. In its centre is the fountain of St. George. The group of statues made of sandstone represents the legendary knight fighting against a dragon. Every building

at Primaciálne námestie deserves attention. The most important of them is the **Stará radnica*** ❸ or the Old Town Hall. Opposite the Primatial Palace is **Nová radnica*** ❷ (the New Town Hall). This modern building replaced the 17th century Jesuit monastery demolished in 1948.

The eastern side of today's Primatial Palace is closed by the buildings, which have their entrances from Uršulínska and Klobučnícka

originated as the street skirting the town walls of the medieval town. It followed the eastern section of the fortifications. Opposite the school standing near the crossroads with Klobučnícka street there is a preserved section of the **town walls*** ❺ from the 15th century. The inner part of the stone wall reaching the height of the neighbouring two-storied house is visible here. Uršulínska ulica street connects Laurinská street with Primatial square and the square of the SNP. The **Ursuline church** and **monastery*** ❻ unifies the eastern row of the Ursuline Street. The Evangelicals built the church in 1640 for their Slovak and Hungarian believers.

streets. Klobučnícka ulica street as we see it now, is a comparatively young street. The dominating building of Klobučnícka street is the Neo Baroque tenement house No. 2 from 1910. In the yard of the smart four-storied house with attic roof is what is called **Hummel's house***** ❹. It is a small and picturesque Renaissance house often denoted as the native house of Johann Nepomuk Hummel (1778-1837). This world famous composer and pianist though, was born in the house, which existed there before. Hummel's house contains now part of the **musical exhibition** of the Municipal Museum, which documents the life and work of the composer, and the musical history of Bratislava.

Around today's Nedbalova ulica street, perpendicular to Klobučnícka, was the Jewish ghetto with a synagogue. Nedbalova ulica, as we know it now,

❶ The painting on the ceiling of the St. Ladislav's chapel ❷ Artisans on the Primaciálne námestie square ❸ Hummel's house ❹ Pedestrian zone on the Primaciálne námestie square

Das haus ob prespurcs

2

The Bratislava Castle

The monumental building of **Bratislava Castle****** that cannot be confused with any other building in the city is visible from a great distance. Certainly every visitor of Bratislava notices the pronounced silhouette similar to an overturned table. The majestic impression is enhanced by the hill it stands on some eighty-five metres above the water level of the Danube.

The castle hill had a special function within the system of Great Moravian fortified

1 Castle of Bratislava in the 14th century **2** Castle of Bratislava
3 Great Moravian basilica **4** Panoramic view of Bratislava

The fortification of the castle hill made use of the defensive system of the previous fortified settlement. In the second

15th century. Generous reconstruction of the castle started in 1423 during the rule of Sigismund of Luxembourg, but it was

settlements. Building activity documented by archaeology took place on the castle hill of Bratislava as early as the 10th century. First there was a pre-Romanesque **stone palace ❶** in the 11th and 12th centuries.

half of the 13th century the castle progressively gained the shape of the Romanesque Arpád period castle, which it kept until the Gothic reconstruction carried out in time of King Sigismund in the first half of the

not finished in time of his death in 1437. The result of this reconstruction was a Gothic castle referred to in literature as a Sigismund's castle. Two semicircular cannon bastions reinforced the castle walls. The northern bastion was

64

called **Luginsland** ❷. Even today it is the dominant architectural element of Bratislava's castle well visible from the Hodžovo or Župné squares. A new entrance to the castle via **Žigmundova brána** ❸ (Sigismund's Gate) was built on the steep slope of the castle hill above the Danube.

Reconstruction of the castle generally referred to as Pálffy's was carried out in the period of the fading Renaissance style. Pálffy's luxurious **castle palace** ❹ was a part of ambitious plan for

reconstruction of the whole castle hill, with the settlement below it included in a massive fort with a complicated system of bastions and ramparts arranged in an irregular seven-pointed star. Out of this extensive project led by the Italian builder J. Priami only a tiny part was made reality. Only two cannon bastions were added to the castle.

A long tunnel was drilled under the south-western one. The tunnel was used as an entrance gate and its name was **Leopoldova**

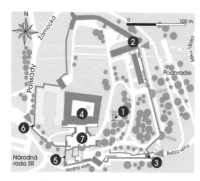

brána ❺ (Leopold's Gate). However, it proved to be an error as it was not conveniently situated and moreover it was rather unattractive from the architectural point of view. A new and more pompous entrance gate was started. Since it was situated on the western edge of the castle hill and as it was on the road from Vienna it acquired the name **Viedenská brána ❻** (Vienna gate). This gate similar to Antique triumphal arches

was ceremoniously opened on the occasion of Charles III's coronation in 1712. It has remained the main entrance to the area of Bratislava Castle until today.

The last stage of big building adjustments of the Pressburg Castle was accomplished under the

❶ The Rococo stairway of the castle palace **❷** Courtyard of the castle palace **❸** View from the Coronation tower **❹** Sigismund's Gate **❺** Lugisland Bastion

orders of Queen Maria Theresia. The works pursuing the project of reconstruction as presented by the imperial architects J. N. Jadot, G. B. Martinelli and N. Pacassi started in 1755. The castle now called **Theresian** was prepared to serve the royal court

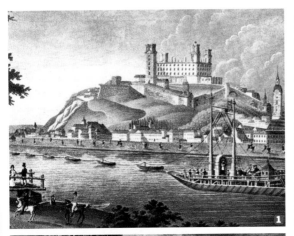

were built and on the southern terrace a kind of **courtyard of honour ❼** was created.

The most interesting building though was that of the Theresianum built next to the eastern side of the palace in 1768. This lovely Rococo palace was the seat of the Governor, Prince Albert, who acquired the office after he married Archduchess Maria Christina, daughter of Queen Maria Theresia. In May 1811, a devastating fire burst out in the castle and soon spread to the Podhradie or the settlement below the castle. For the next hundred and fifty years the people had to tolerate the sad picture of the destroyed castle on top of the hill, a vanishing symbol of the city's past glory. Some parts of the castle are open to the public now. They contain permanent exhibitions of the **Slovak National Museum**.

in 1765. The obvious and intentional disproportion between the dreary exterior and impressive interior was again applied. Money not spent on the outer appearance was invested in the interior of the castle. The simplicity of the outer facades complied with the canons of Classicising Baroque. In front of the southern facade a couple of Baroque guard houses

❶ Castle at the beginning of the 19th century ❷ The burning Castle in 1811 ❸ Castle now

The western part of the Old Town

The western part of the Old Town is quite different from the other parts. It spreads over the foothills of the Little Carpathians and its urban fabric consists predominantly of family houses. On a flat hill at its south-eastern edge is the Bratislava Castle and on its eastern and southern slopes is **Podhradie**, the historic settlement below the castle.

Several buildings in Beblavá, Židovská, Mikulášska streets and at the stairway called Zámocké schody deserve attention. Let us look at them and start with the house at the lower end of Židovská ulica street, which is rightly, considered one of the most beautiful in Bratislava. It is the impressive **Dom u dobrého pastiera*** (House of the Good Shepherd) and its conspicuously slender construction makes it the best specimen of small-scale Rococo architecture in Bratislava. Its name derives from a tiny statue of Christ – Good Shepherd

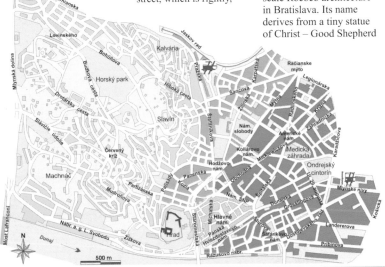

– standing on its corner. It was built in 1760. Since 1975 the House of the Good Shepherd has sheltered the exposition of historic clocks of the Municipal Museum. Also the collection of portable sun dials from the 16th – 18th centuries is interesting. **Zsigray's curia**** standing at the opposite end of Židovská street (No 17) offers the opportunity to see the exhibits of the **Museum of Jewish Culture in Slovakia** explaining the history of the Jewish community of Bratislava and Slovakia. On the slope of the castle hill above Mikulášska ulica street there

stands the **St. Nicholas' church**. The church has belonged to the followers of the Eastern Orthodox Church since 1950.

Beblavého ulica street climbs the castle hill from the corner of the House of the Good Shepherd. It was the shortest possible connection between the castle and St. Martin's Minster. As the famous Hungarian poet Sándor Petöfi lived in its upper part the street bore his name for some time. Today it offers an opportunity to sit and chat in pleasant stylish little cafés and restaurants in venerable houses from the 18th century. At the lower end of Beblavého street stands the **Late Baroque house No. 1**** from the late 18th century. It contains the **Museum of crafts** exhibiting works of artisans made of glass, porcelain, various types of jewels, toys and liturgical objects. In the upper part of Zámocké schody stairs are two

Renaissance houses from the beginning of the 17th century.

The round hills of Bratislava spreading

from Štefánikova ulica street up to Dolná Mlynská dolina valley were for centuries a viticultural landscape with

scattered little huts. This attractive locality acquired a new function only in the first half of the 20th century. The footpaths between the plots

changed to streets built up with elegant villas; the property of the Bratislava's privileged class and social elite. The locality is the most expensive and most luxurious quarter of the city. It main street is Mudroňova ulica street, originally called Kaiserweg or the Emperor's Road. Next to the castle on the

1 The House of the Good Shepherd **2** Façade of the Museum of crafts **3** Jewish Museum **4** Rybné námestie square 100 years ago **5** Podhradie today

Vodný vrch hill is the modern **building of the National Council of the Slovak Republic****. It was opened in May 1994 and the Slovak Parliament moved here from its old seat in Župné námestie. The new buildings of Parliament also include the popular Parlamentka restaurant with a terrace above the Danube offering a wide view of the city.

At the upper end of Mudroňova in the north-east is the **Murmannova výšina***

hill with the **House of Ekoiuventa*** built in 1952, colloquially called "Michurin" (surname of Soviet scientist known for bold experimentation with plants). The building is a perfect sample of what is called Stalinist architecture. It is still serving its original purpose – it provides space for children's leisure activities.

Stará vinárska ulica street starting nearby leads to the neighbouring height (252 m) with the **monument Slavín**** and military

cemetery where 6,845 Soviet soldiers who died while liberating Bratislava by the end of April of 1945 are buried.

1 and **3** Castle of Bratislava seen from below Slavín **2** Hills of Bratislava in the 19th century **4** Slavín **5** The tablet at Slavín

The northern part of the Old Town

The quarters in the north of the historic centre of Bratislava are full of contrasts. There are busy wide streets and romantic narrow alleys. One can walk in wide squares and pleasant parks. Venerable buildings breathing with history stand side by side with modern buildings. In the northern part of the centre are the buildings of the government, ministries, the Presidential Palace and the seats of many other central administrative bodies and institutions. The main railway station in the northern centre is the place of the first contact with the city for visitors to Bratislava.

Several squares originated around the disappeared town walls. One of them is Župné námestie square connected with the contiguous Hurbanovo square in the east. In the Middle Ages it was the site of the settlement of St. Michael, which later developed into a suburb. In time of Turkish wars the aldermen themselves decided to demolish the suburbs for the sake of better control over the immediate space beyond the town walls. Such was the destiny of the St. Michael suburb including its Gothic

1 Presidential Palace **2** Portal of the Trinity church **3** Trinity church

church bearing the name of the same patron saint. It was pulled down in 1529. The **Trinitarian** order later built one of the most beautiful Baroque **churches***** in the town on its ruins.

In the time when this church was consecrated, construction of the **Trinitarian monastery** on the neighbouring plot of the disappeared cemetery was going on. When the Trinitarians left, the building was given to the county administration. But it was not suitable for the offices.

It was pulled down and in its place a new **Župný dom**** (County House) for the Pressburg county administration office was built in 1844.

In the years 1939-1994 the Slovak legislative bodies held their sessions in the Župný dom and after 1945 it became the seat of the Slovak National Council (in 1992 renamed to the National Council of the Slovak Republic). Since 1994 the sessions of the Slovak Parliament are held in a new building on the Vodný vrch hill. The shortest western side of

the triangular Župné námestie coincides with the facade of the **Capuchin church**** consecrated to St. Stephen of Hungary. The Capuchin church was consecrated by Bishop L. A. Erdödy of Nitra in 1717. Part of the church was pulled down and rebuilt in 1735. The space in front of the Capuchin church is adorned by the **Morový stĺp** (Plaque pillar).

The environs of **Panenská ulica** street belonged to the Pressburg Evangelicals or Lutherans since the late 17th century. They lost their two churches in the town centre in 1672 and a special imperial commission prohibited the Evangelical service in the

inner town. They were ordered out to the northern suburb, a scarcely built area between the Suché mýto and Kozia gates. Construction of the **Big Evangelical Church**** on Panenská ulica took place in years 1774-1777. The architect M. Walch tried to imitate the original German Evangelical Church, which used to stand near the Old Town Hall. It is built in the Neo-Classical style. The **Small Evangelical Church**** on Panenská stands on the site of the former wooden "articled" church from 1682.

1 The Capuchin church and detail of the pillar in front of it
2 Evangelical Lycée
3 Konventná street

Konventná ulica street is closely associated with Evangelical schooling in Pressburg, the beginnings of which date to 1606. The Evangelical community of Pressburg was one of the largest in Hungary in the early 18th century. It associated about seven thousand believers of the three nationalities. The community invited to its **Lycée****** in Pressburg **Matej Bel** (1684-1749), the former student of this institution in 1714, immediately after the retreat of the plague epidemic. It soon became obvious that

it was a good move. Matej Bel was not only a scientist of world importance, but also a good teacher and educator. He wrote and published text books, adapted the Latin grammar and initiated the publishing of the newspaper *Nova Posoniensia* in Latin. He became the first priest of the German Evangelical Church and the chancellor of the Lycée. For his scientific achievements he was referred to as The Great Ornament of Hungary.

Suché mýto square appeared in the historic documents in 1375 under the name Dauermauth. It was the medieval toll entrance into the inner suburbs through the gate and bridge over the moat. The modern Suché mýto is completely different in comparison with the past. Demolition of old houses and reconstruction of the transport system connected Suché mýto with what is now Hodžovo námestie square into one big open space framed by modern buildings. One of them is the Crowne Plaza Hotel on the south-eastern side of the square. The hotel built according to design of the architect J. Hauskrecht has

a capacity of 450 beds and was opened in 1988. The dominant building of Hodžovo námestie square is the **Presidential Palace***** built after 1760 as the garden palace of Anton Grassalkovich. The building of this wonderful Rococo palace was outside the town and it was placed between the garden of the summer Archbishop's Palace and the town. The central architectural element of the palace is the pavilion in its middle from which two palace wings spread. In front of the palace is a courtyard skirted by an impressive fence with a pair of gilded metal gates. The buildings on Štefánikova

1 The corner of Štefánikova and Tolstého streets **2** Matej Bel **3** Detail of the gate of Presidential Palace **4** Presidential Palace **5** The Fount of Peace **6** Garden of Presidential Palace

ulica street and the contiguous streets are mainly smart residences. On the eastern side of the street and neighbouring with Grassalkovich's garden is the **Karácsonyi Palace*** (house No. 2) with the Neo Baroque facade. It was built by the end of the 19th century and later rebuilt into an administrative building. Between Spojná and Leškova streets are several luxurious family villas. Villas cover the view of an extensive **park**, which is closed to the public. It belongs to the area of the Office of the Government of the

Slovak Republic. The park occupies the site of the former Archbishop's garden, which stretched from today's Štefánikova up to Námestie slobody square. The summer **Archbishop's Palace** on the upper part of Námestie slobody square lived through the good and bad times together with the garden. Today it is the seat of the **Office of the Government of the Slovak Republic****.

1 Office of the Government of the SR **2** National Bank **3** Bratislava today **4** Námestie SNP square at the beginning of the 20th century **5** Old Market Hall 100 years ago and now

The eastern part of the Old Town

▦ This part of the centre attracts the shoppers and visitors of Bratislava, because it has the majority anti-Nazi uprisings in Europe which burst out in Central Slovakia at the end of August 1944. The **monument to the SNP*** with a trio of big bronze statues by Ján Kulich on the lower end of the side bordering with historical part of the city is the building known under the name **Manderla** (No. 23). This eleven-storied **house** is the first of Bratislava's

of shops, shopping centres, and department stores. The busiest spot is the **Námestie Slovenského národného povstania** (SNP) or Square of the Slovak National Uprising. It commemorates one of the biggest national is associated with this significant event of the modern Slovak history.

In the upper part of the square is the spacious building of the Old or **Main Post Office** (houses No. 34-36). The last building of the SNP square "skyscrapers", and for long the tallest building in the city. It was built in 1935 for the rich businessman trading in meat Rudolf Manderla.

The dominating building of the north-western side of the triangle-shaped

building of the square though is the **church and monastery of the Merciful Brothers**** (Milosrdných bratov) in the north-east. The Špitálska ulica street starts in the SNP square and heads to the north-east. Its name is linked to the fact it has been the site of several hospitals since the Middle Ages. As early as 1307 the municipal council agreed with the Antonite Order about administration of the hospital built on plots east of the town. The municipal hospital of St. Anton stood opposite today's St. Ladislav's church. Next to the hospital of St. Ladislav was a cemetery with a chapel. The central architecture

SNP square is the Neo Romanesque **Calvinist church***with a tall tower. It was designed by the architect F. Wimmer and built in 1913. The biggest

of the complex is **St. Ladislav's church****. Some metres away from St. Ladislav's church are the **Elizabethan church and monastery****. The

1 Manderla **2** Lion's fount **3** St. Ladislav's church **4** Comenius University **5** Elizabethan church **6** Duck fount

new quarter lying next to the Starý most bridge also got a new church in 1913 thanks to Countess G. M. Szapáryová. It was a beautiful one, still to be seen on Bezručova ulica street, and known by the natives as Modrý kostolík or the **Blue Church***** (Church of St. Elisabeth). It is a wonderful example of the Art Noveau style in sacred architecture.

Šafárikovo námestie square originated after 1891, when the first fixed bridge was built over the Danube. Varied buildings frame Šafárikovo námestie square. One of the most recent is the **Comenius University*** (house No. 5). Architect F. Krupka built it in 1930 for the stock exchange following the winning design. Today it is the seat of the Faculty of Law of Comenius University.

Bratislava's embankment

Today the area around the embankment of the city between the historic centre and the left bank of the Danube are the favourite routes of walks, occasional visits to a museum or gallery or meetings in one of the boat hotel restaurants on the river. The route starting at the Old Town and heading up stream toward the Botanical Garden is perhaps the most popular one for a Sunday afternoon walk.

The first part of the route runs along the **Fajnorovo nábrežie** embankment bearing the name of the Evangelical bishop and writer Dušan Fajnor (1876-1933). Even before the origin of embankment the oldest of the existing four Bratislava bridges over

2

1 The Ganymede`s fount

2 Slovak National Museum

3 The port of Bratislava at the beginning of the 20th century

3

the Danube, now called the **Starý most****(Old Bridge), was built. The bridge opened a day before the New Year's Eve of 1890 and remained the only over the Danube in Bratislava for another 83 years. In the space between Fajnorovo and Vajanského nábrežie embankments is the building of the **Slovak National Museum**** built in the years 1924-1928 for the branch of the Museum of Agriculture. Now the Museum contains exhibitions of natural history. The monument to the Czech and Slovak statehood adorns the space in front of the Museum. It was ceremoniously introduced to the public on October 28th of 1988.

A bronze **statue of lion*** leaning on the state symbol of the former Czechoslovakia stands on the almost fifteen metres tall pylon.

Vajanského nábrežie embankment bears the name of the Slovak politician, journalist, and writer, Svetozár Hurban Vajanský (1847-1916). The most interesting building on Vajanského embankment from the architectural point of view is the **Jurenák Palace*** (house No. 4). In this Neo Classical house of burgher K. Jurenák, composer Johannes Brahms (1833-1897) stayed during his visit to Pressburg. Next to the building of the Slovak Philharmonic Orchestra

the embankment **opens onto Námestie Ľ. Štúra square** skirted by elegant buildings. Until 1939 it bore the name Coronation square as it used to be the setting of the final ceremony of coronations.

The short Mostová ulica street connects Námestie Ľ. Štúra with Hviezdoslavovo námestie squares. The street originated after the regulation of the river. Originally it headed to the pontoon bridge of Carolina Augusta over the Danube what explains the name of the street. Historic documents quote that there used to be the Zum König von Ungarn Hotel (King of Hungary Hotel) on this street. Now the principal landmark of

this street is the **Reduta**** building. It was built in 1911-1915 as designed by the Budapest architects M. Komor and D. Jakab. The monumental silhouette of this elegant building tries to copy the basic shape of the older building of the provincial granary which was built here in the years 1773-1774. The Reduta is now the seat of the **Slovak Philharmonic Orchestra**. Occasionally it hosts the top domestic and foreign musical ensembles and outstanding soloists of classic music. The concert season culminates in the Bratislava Music Festival organized in Autumn every year.

The **Rázusovo nábrežie** embankment running from Námestie Ľudovíta Štúra to the **New Bridge** was

1 Coronation hill 2 Building of Reduta taken from Námestie Ľ. Štúra square 3 Námestie Ľ. Štúra square 100 years ago

created in the 18th century in the place where there was a fishermen's village before. Building in this space started in the mid-19th century and the embankment was called Dunajské. Now it bears the mane of the Slovak poet, writer and politician Martin Rázus (1888-1937). The oldest building on the Rázusovo embankment is the compound of former barracks called **Vodné kasárne**. The building was adapted in the years 1949-1951 for the **Slovak National Gallery**** (SNG). The collections of the SNG include the most important works of the Slovak fine arts since the 13th century until the present time and examples of European arts from the 15th to 18th centuries. Beside the permanent collections, interesting temporary exhibitions are sometimes held.

Hviezdoslavovo námestie square is a wonderful and lively place. The most impressive building on the Hviezdoslavovo námestie square is the **Slovak National Theatre*****. The elegant eclectic theatre building has adorned the city since 1886. The SND put on dramas and operas until 1955 when the drama ensemble

1 Slovak National Theatre **2** Slovak National Gallery

moved to a separate new building on Laurinská street leaving the stage of the SND to ballet and opera only. The SND hosted some important figures of world opera and ballet. It was also here where several opera stars of Slovak origin started their careers: Peter Dvorský, Edita Grúberová, and Lucia Poppová.

The space in front of the SND building is adorned by **Ganymedes' fountain****. The fountain is the present of the First Pressburg Savings Bank. Ganymedes' fountain is not the only artistic work on the rectangular area of Hviezdoslavovo námestie square. There is also the **monument*** to the poet P. O. Hviezdoslav with

its fountain standing here since 1937. The south-eastern part of Hviezdoslavovo námestie square widens into a small squarish area with a park. This was the plot originally reserved for the church of the St. Augustín of Notre Dame female order. Only the chancel with a little porch added in the 19th century was built. In the interior of the presbytery a ceiling fresco by the Baroque painter P. Troger survived. In front of the unfinished building stands a little wooden tower. The former monastery of the Notre Dame order built in 1754 as the front wing of the building is now the Church school of Mother Alexia. The park with the adjacent area of

ÖNTÖTTE BESCHORNER A.M.

1 The clock next to Carlton Hotel **2** Hviezdoslavovo nám. square **3** Ganymedes' fount **4** Monument of Hviezdoslav **5** Slovak National Theatre

Hviezdoslavovo námestie square was the place where the "candle demonstration" took place on March 25th 1988. The security units using water cannons cruelly attacked the calmly protesting and praying believers with lit candles.

TRIPS STARTING FROM THE OLD TOWN

The **Botanical garden*** on Botanická ulica street is owned and administered by the Faculty of Nature Science of Comenius University. It lies close to the Danube, west from the **Lafranconi bridge***. It was founded in the years 1942-1943 on an area of 50.7 hectares. When the green house was constructed the garden acquired many tropical plant species. The pride of the green house is a little lake with precious water plants and numerous collections of cactuses. Today there are about 5,000 foreign plant species including 650 wood species. The botanical garden is interesting in every season, but it is most beautiful in the spring when the flowers are in full

1 Castle of Devín **2** Dinopark at the ZOO
3 The bear at the ZOO

bloom. In Mlynská dolina valley in the neighbourhood of the Slovak Television is the **Zoo**** of Bratislava. It was opened to the public in 1960. Its original area was 9 hectares. Later it was enlarged to the present 90 hectares and contains more than 200 animal species.

The National Nature Reserve of **Devínska Ko-byla**** is a unique locality of special fauna and flora. It lies in part of the Devínske Karpaty mountains on an area 101 hectares between Devínska Nová Ves, Dúbravka and Devín; 234 species of mushrooms, 110 species of lichens, 100 species of mosses, and 1,100 plant species confirm the originality of this place. Xerophytes and thermophiles with precious and protected plant species and animals live on the southern and south-western slopes of Devínska Kobyla. The forests on the south-western slopes are the remains of the original thermopile oak growths. An **instructive path** leading through the reserve provides visitors with information about the occurrence of special vegetation and wild life. It has got seven stops with information panels. The most interesting locality of the National Nature Reserve Devínska Kobyla is the sand profile on the **Sandberg**** mountain. There are rock remains of

1 Sandberg **2** The Morava river
3 Virgin tower **4** Spring in Devín

the Tertiary sea with horizontal layers, the age of which is estimated at 14 to 16 million years. Another **instructive route** was prepared in 1996 over the flood plain of the Morava which runs along the river Morava from Devín to Devínska Nová Ves and ends in Vysoká pri Morave (outside Bratislava). The 23 km long route has 16 information boards.

The urban district **DEVÍN** (population 900) lies below the Devín Castle at the confluence of the Danube and Morava. Devín is ten kilometres away from Bratislava. The village with castle lies on the spot where the Danube enters the Devínska brána (Devín Gate).

Devín Castle**** standing on a massive rock hill above the confluence of the Danube and Morava is an unusually impressive landmark. Its ground plan is very irregular. Today we enter the castle through the western **Moravian Gate ❶**. The southern gate protected by a pair of semicircular bastions was built in the 15th century on an older Great Moravian rampart. Close behind the gate and on

the right side of the path is a precious archaeological monument from the Roman period of Devín's history. The ground plan of the **remains of a bulky stone building** from the 4th century suggests a Classical tomb. Fragments of wall with preserved plasters up to 85 cm tall and the original floor were found there. Left from the path and near the Moravská brána gate Old Slavic graves from the 10th and 11th centuries were found.

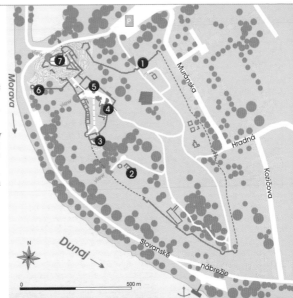

1 Castle of Devín today **2** The Danube below Devín **3** Landscape park of Bratislava **4** Kamzík

Near the well is also a terrace with view of the abandoned **amphitheatre**, the Danube and the mountain of Braunsberg in Austria. In the wonderful setting above the bicolour confluence of the Danube and Morava an elegant tower with battlements stands out. It is the **Virgin tower ❻**. A bridge over a moat and stairs lead to the **top platform ❼** with

The path divides into two on the ridge of the castle hill. The left branch leads to the place where stood a **Great Moravian church ❷** in the 9th century. One can see its rectangular ground plan with an apsid. The first branch of the path leads to the conserved ruins of the middle and upper part of the **medieval castle**, which was smaller than the Great Moravian fort. In the first half of the 15th century the Gothic **Garay palace ❸** with two stories

was built and the **Renaissance palace ❹** and fortifications were added in the 16th century. Some vaulted spaces of this palace are today used for exhibitions. The origin of the 55 metres deep **castle well ❺**, which is on the courtyard of the middle castle, is linked to the period when Garray was the owner ot the castle.

remnants of a guard tower from the 13th century rebuilt in the 15th century with panoramic view of the surroundings.

More than a half of the area of the urban district of Nové mesto is occupied by the landscape park called **Bratislavský lesný park**. This indeed large (17 square kilometres) recreation area in the territory of Bratislava are the forests of the southern part of the Little Carpathians. This part consists mostly of meadows and broad-leaved forest, which offer possibilities of relaxing in a pleasant setting. The area has numerous marked hiking footpaths and tourist amenities. The massive mountain of **Kamzík*** (439 m) in the southern part of

the Little Carpathians is a place frequently visited by Bratislava trippers. It is easily accessible by an asphalt road from Koliba. However, the main tourist attraction of Kamzík is the 200 metres tall **TV tower** built in 1974 on its top. The revolving restaurant on top of the tower offers panoramic view of the environs reaching, in fair weather as far as the Neusiedel lake and the Alps in Austria.

North of Nové Mesto is the urban district **RAČA** (population 20,150). It is about 8 kilometre away from the city centre. In the west it includes part of the forested massive of the Little Carpathians and in the east it borders on Vajnory. The history of Rača is closely linked to its **viticultural traditions**. The local vineyards are referred to in the oldest historic document from 1237. A visit to Rača is an excellent opportunity to see a typical Little Carpathian viticultural village in its almost intact form.

The urban district **VAJNORY** (population 3,850) is on the north-western edge of Bratislava, about 10 km away from the city centre. Although Vajnory became part of the city, it preserved its traditional rural character. The oldest peasant houses of Vajnory are from the early 19th century. One

1 Rača **2** Vintage in Rača **3** Folk costumes of Vajnory **4** Gothic tower in the Sad Janka Kráľa **5** Danubiana Gallery **6** Manor house in Rusovce

101

of the Vajnory houses on Roľnícka ulica street was adapted as an ethnographic exhibition in 1966. The **Folk House of Vajnory** (No. 185) is not only a representative example of traditional dwelling of a vintner of Vajnory, it also offers wonderful products of folk painters in its interior.

RUSOVCE (population 1,900) is the biggest of the three urban districts of the other bank of the Danube lying south of Petržalka. Rusovce is a very old community. Though its territory was settled already in the Older Bronze Age it became most notable in the first four centuries when the northern frontiers of the Roman Empire moved to the middle section of the Danube. The territory of today's

Rusovce found itself in the Roman province of Pannonia administered

from Carnuntum. Romans built there the military camp of **Gerulata** as a

part of the Limes Romanus defensive system, securing the northern limit of the Empire against the raids of German tribes. The antique history of Rusovce is documented in the exhibition of the **Municipal Museum Múzeum antiky – Gerulata** (open only in summer).

The architectural feature of Rusovce is the Neo-Classical **manor house** built in 1840 on the site of an older manor house from 1521. The manor house acquired its attractive facade by application of the Roman-ticizing style of what is called the Windsor type imitating the English Gothic. It has towers, battlements and a central risalite with terrace. In front of the manor house is the **statue of a lion** standing on a pillar.

Accommodation

Crowne Plaza
Hodžovo nám. 2
☎ 5934 8111
www.ichotelsgroup.com

**Radisson SAS
Carlton Hotel**
Hviezdoslavovo nám. 3
☎ 5939 0000
www.radissonsas.com

Hotel Danube
Rybné nám. 1
☎ 5934 0000
www.hoteldanube.com

Hotel Devín
Riečna 4
☎ 5443 3640
www.hoteldevin.sk

Hotel Perugia
Zelená 5
☎ 5443 1818
www.perugia.sk

Hotel Marrol's
Tobrucká 4
☎ 5778 4600
www.hotelmarrols.sk

Hotel Dukla
Dulovo nám. 1
☎ 5596 8922
www.hoteldukla.sk

PRACTICAL INFORMATION

Accommodation

Hotels in Bratislava are comparatively expensive. As their number is limited, they are almost always fully booked above all in holiday season and in time of fairs or conferences of national and international scope. Old historical hotels in the town centre are now restored and together with modern hotels they joined the standard European establishments. Cheaper accommodation is normally to be found farther from the centre or out of the town.

Officially, hotels are classified into five categories. In order to offer a simpler orientation concerning hotels, this guidebook offers the classification of accommodating facilities in the Old Town into two groups – the luxurious four-star hotels and standard three-star hotels. Chosen establishment with the best reputation and located in the hinterland of the Old Town are included.

Luxurious hotels offer modern technical equipment

and an exclusive interior. All rooms have their bathrooms and lavatories; they contain a colour TV set with satellite or cable receiver, a radio, refrigerator, telephone and a vault. The prices of the room also cover the breakfast in form of a buffet. Luxurious hotels provide almost all usual services including those of personal nature and special services for travelling salesmen and marketing services.

The **Radisson SAS Carlton** Hotel, the oldest, recently restored hotel with the best position in the town centre offers a wide scale of services including sauna, gymnasium, fitness centre, congress halls, a restaurant with excellent menus and the underground parking. Swimming pool is the only facility it lacks to be classified into the five-star hotel category. The **Devín**

Hotel is also among the first class accommodation facilities of Bratislava. It is situated on the embankment of the Danube in the historical centre. It is an older building, which provides the best quality relaxation centres including the swimming pool and squash ground. The hotel possesses the distinguished French restaurant with a coffeehouse, bar and congress centre and luxurious lounge. Both hotels have become symbols of Bratislava that are best appreciated by clients who prefer a high style and good locality.

The **Danube** Hotel with an above-standard level of provided services (car rent, guarded parking, garage, shops, hairdresser's, conferences hall for 300 persons, etc.) also stands on the bank of the Danube. It is the favourite of foreigners because of its excellent position in the town centre. The **Crowne Plaza** Hotel is ideal for service or business stays and it is situated near the Presidential Palace in the centre. It contains three restaurants, coffeehouses, a casino, bar, nightclub, fitness centre, swimming pool, sauna, solarium and congress hall. **Perugia** is a smaller cosy hotel standing right within the pedestrian zone in the Old Town. It offers a pleasant atmosphere and excellent cooking. The retro-atmosphere of the beginning of the 20th century of the **Marrol's** Hotel, the one with perhaps the most beautiful interior decoration, attracts not only businessmen but also clients who love a good-quality and classic treatment. Its Italian restaurant Messina complements the comfort and cultivated elegance of the hotel.

Our first category also includes the two hotels situated in the hinterland of the Old Town. One of them is the **Holiday Inn** Hotel in the eastern part of Bratislava, which is known above all

Hotel Tatra
Nám. 1. mája 5
☎ 5927 2111
www.hoteltatra.sk

Film Hotel
Vysoká 27
☎ 5293 1600
www.filmhotel.sk

Hotel No 16
Partizánska 16/a
☎ 5441 1672
www.hotelno16.sk

Holiday Inn
Bajkalská 25/a
☎ 4824 5111
www.holidayinn.sk

City Hotel Bratislava
Seberíniho 9
☎ 4341 1592
www.cityhotelbratislava.sk

Hotel Barónka
Mudrochova 2
☎ 4488 2089
www.baronka.sk

Hotel Hradná brána
Slovanské nábr. 15
☎ 6010 2511
www.hotelhb.sk

Hotel Ibis
Zámocká 38
☎ 5929 2000
www.ibiz-bratislava.sk

Hotel Arcus
Moskovská 5
☎ 5557 2522
www.hotelarcus.sk

Penzión Grémium
Gorkého 11
☎ 5413 1026
www.gremium.sk

Botel Gracia
Rázusovo nábr.
☎ 5443 2132
www.botel-gracia.sk

Botel Fairway
Nábr. arm. gen.
L. Svobodu
☎ 5441 4442
www.fairway.sk

Hotel Club
Odbojárov 3
☎ 4463 5737
www.hotelclub.sk

Hotel Sorea
Kráľovské údolie 6
☎ 5441 4442
www.sorea.sk

among businessman for its congress facilities and quality catering. Another simple and modern hotel is the one constructed in the western part of the town, right below the Devín Castle – the **Hradná brána** Hotel. It is sought out by clients who want to spend their nights outside the busy town centre.

The category of **standard hotels** covers the majority of three-star hotels with smart, comfortable and standard equipment, a wide variety of hotel services for personal or professional needs of their guests. There are bathrooms and lavatories to all rooms and they also contain colour TV sets, radios, refrigerators and telephones.

One of them, the **Ibis** Hotel (French hotel chain of Accor) is situated below the Castle of Bratislava. The offer of its services suits best the travelling businessmen. The quiet **Arcus** Hotel stands within a short walk from the town centre near the park of Medická záhrada. It has a family atmosphere and although it has no restaurant, it is appreciated by those who do not like large spaces of giant hotels. In the calm and the best residential quarter of Bratislava there is the small and intimate No. 16 Hotel, frequented by foreign visitors. The **Film Hotel** where each room is dedicated to some famous film star is on the Vysoká St. in the centre. If you visit the hotel restaurant you may pass by Marilyn Monroe for instance and the dishes bear names of films or film stars. The reconstructed **Sorea** Hotel standing above the Danube River is also one of Bratislava`s hotels. The boat hotels **Gracia** and **Fairway** provide additional beds and their reputation is flawless. The **Tatra** Hotel near the Presidential Palace complement the offer of standard hotels in the centre of Bratislava. But this category also includes three

CROWNE PLAZA

BRATISLAVA

Crowne Plaza Hotel Bratislava is the first class de luxe hotel, situated in the centre of the Capital, right next to the Presidential Palace. It offers comfortable accommodation in its 223 rooms, 14 modern conference rooms with the total area of 1200 m² and the top technical equipment and excellent cuisine. Eating in the Crowne Plaza Bratislava is an unforgettable experience. The offer of the new luxurious fitness centre also includes the swimming pool, sauna, solarium and massages.

Crowne Plaza Bratislava
Hodžovo nám. 2, 816 25 Bratislava 1
☎ +421 2 5934 8111, fax: +421 2 5443 3265
e-mail: cp.bratislava@ichotelsgroup.com
www.ichotelsgroup.com, www.cpbratislava.com

Penzión Zlatá Noha

The Zlatá Noha boarding house is situated not far away from the historical centre of Bratislava, at the urban district of Koliba. As it stands on top of the hill it offers a wonderful panoramic view of the city. It also invites to horse riding in the natural forest that surrounds the premises of the Zlatá noha boarding house.

The Zlatá Noha boarding house
Bellova 2/a, 831 01 Bratislava
☎ +421 2 5477 4922, fax: +421 2 5465 1848, 0903 789 179, 0903 421 075, zlatanoha@stonline.sk

Restaurants

Preégo
Žilinská 4
☎ 0903 246 226

Zichy
Ventúrska 9
☎ 5441 8551

Reduta
Mostová 3
☎ 5443 5257

Savoyka
Obchodná 2
☎ 5443 2002

Slovenská reštaurácia
Hviezdoslavovo nám. 20
☎ 5441 6442

U Vodníka
Lovinského 11
☎ 5477 4277

Tempus Fugit
Sedlárska 5
☎ 5441 4357

Ludwig
Ventúrska 7
☎ 5464 8284

Traja mušketieri
Sládkovičova 7
☎ 5443 0019

Al Dente
Hodžovo nám. 3
☎ 5464 8057

Peoples Lounge Restaurant
Gorkého 1
☎ 5464 0777

hotels lying in the hinterland of the Old Town. It is the **Dukla** Hotel situated east of the centre. Since it has been reconstructed it offers accommodation at different prices to suit all kinds of clients. The **Club Hotel**, one of the Czech hotel chain Orea Hotels is also recommended for businessman and tourists. It is situated next to the National Tennis Centre. The **Barónka** Hotel stands, rather retired from the noisy centre, in the north-eastern part of Bratislava next to the vineyards of the urban district Rača.

Food and drinks

The simplest way how to find out about the character of any town is to try the local food. Bratislava offers many options and opportunities. The original cuisine of Bratislava is varied and tasty thanks to the effects of the surrounding Slovak and European regions. The diet in Slovakia normally observes the following rules: breakfast is rather light, the lunch is served comparatively early (between 11 a.m and 1 p.m. hours) and it consists of two dishes, the soup and the "main" dish. The dinner is served from 5 p.m. and it is substantial. However, many restaurants offer meals anytime until late hours. The following details are also typical: aperitif is served first, beer, wine or soft drinks are drank with meal, festive

meals are often accompanied by champagne. Coffee or a glass of cognac is taken after dessert. Fast food establishments (McDonald`s) that have sprung in Bratislava recently cannot change these eating habits of the locals.

The local specialties are also interesting. Although restaurants offer international menus there is almost always a typical Slovak dish on their menu. It is for instance, the soup with dumpling, goulash or the carp á la miller. The following restaurants, wine cellars or coffeehouses are located in the Old Town and they enjoy the best reputation.

The Slovak and central European cuisine

Those who want to try something special in nice and quiet environment should drop in the **Preégo** restaurant located in the rear part of the Radio Pyramid in the centre of the town. Its modern and cultivated

interior attracts above all businessmen. One of the best establishments of the town suitable for celebration of special occasions such as anniversaries is the **Zichy** restaurant in the historical core. It is one of the best due to its special menu. The Baroque and Rococo atmosphere of Mozart's time can one find in the luxurious restaurant of **Reduta,** which offers Austrian-Hungarian menu complemented with international cuisine. All meals are not only tasty but also gratifying to sight. The **Savoy** restaurant is nearby and its flawless service complements the pleasing atmosphere.

The **Slovak restaurant** in the traditional folk style with an authentic wooden interior and typical Slovak meals from different regions is in the Hviezdoslavovo námestie square. Its long menu offers a wide choice of quality meals such as "kapustnica" – soup made of sour cabbage, bean or mushroom soups, potato dumpling, and a wide assortment of fishmeals. The **Gazdovský dvor** of the Perugia Hotel is the restaurant based in Hungarian meals. One can enjoy Hungarian meals, such as "halászlé" (fish soup), different kinds of goulash, hot specialities made of quality meats in the stylish atmosphere.

Fans of fish meals will certainly go to building of **U Vodníka** restaurant with excellent fish meals, including many variants of carp and trout and sea food. The **Tempus fugit** is the restaurant in one of the reconstructed 15th century houses in the centre, which also offers many fish meals and steaks.

Exotic and international cuisine

Those who prefer genuine French cuisine should visit the **French restaurant** of the Devín Hotel. The perfectly prepared meals can be accompanied by older French wine served at an indeed decent level. The restaurant **Ludwig** in the town centre or the stylish restaurant of **Three Musketeers** with the atmosphere of the medieval rural inn also offer French dishes and a wide assortment of excellent French wines. The Italian restaurant **Messina** in the Marrol's hotel offers genuine Italian and hand-made pasta and the best Italian wines.

Paparazzi
Laurinská 1
☎ 5464 7971

Le Monde
Ventúrska 1
☎ 5922 7518

Chez David
Zámocká 13/a
☎ 54413824

Jasmín
Seberíniho 1
☎ 4341 1951

Kikaku sushi bar
Gorkého 6
☎ 5443 4783

Tokyo-sushi bar
Panská 27
☎ 5443 4982

Film restaurant
Vysoká 27
☎ 5293 2794

Grémium
Gorkého 11
☎ 5413 1026

Hacienda Mexicana
Sedlárska 6
☎ 0904/556 886

Caribic´s
Žižkova 1/A
☎ 5441 8334

Bagls
Obchodná 2
☎ 5441 0360

Biela pani
Jozefská 11
☎ 5443 5034

Brit
Krížna 23
☎ 5556 7770

Domenico café restaurant
Nám. Ľ. Štúra 4
☎ 5464 0167

Modrá hviezda
Beblavého 14
☎ 5443 2747

Prašná bašta
Zámočnícka 11
☎ 5443 4957

Trafená hus
Šafárikovo nám. 7
☎ 5292 5473

Mezzo Mezzo
Rybárska brána 9
☎ 5443 4393

Medusa
Michalská 21
☎ 5464 7344

Archa
Uršulínska 6
☎ 5443 0865

Flavors
Laurinská 3
☎ 5443 0676

McDonald´s
Gorkého 1
☎ 54 431 520
Obchodná 58
☎ 52 731 328
Nám. SNP 14
☎ 52 921 927

It is an ideal place to relax in the cultivated atmosphere of the hotel. **Al Dente** is another restaurant with prevailing Italian dishes. Its location in the Tatracentre next to the Presidential Palace predestines it for business lunch or dinner. The typical place for meetings and business meals is the **Paparazzi** restaurant in the town centre, with a wide choice of Italian dishes.

The menu of the attractive **Le Monde** restaurant is a good guide over the Scandinavian, Mediterranean or Asian dishes and the restaurant of **Peoples Lounge** standing next to the Opera House or the **Romeo e Guilietta** in the Danube Hotel also prepare a varied scale of meals. **Chez David** stands next to the Castle. The guests enjoy here a high quality of kosher dishes of the original Jewish cuisine.

One can also taste the Thai, Chinese or Japanese meals in Bratislava. The **Jasmín** restaurant below the Castle of Bratislava is the best for Chinese food while the **Kikaku sushi bar** is specialist for the original Japanese and Thai food. Seafood is served in the **Caribic's** restaurant on the Danube embankment.

Pizzerias
Pizzerias of Bratislava are the favourite places to take lunch or a quick meal.

There are several of them in the centre. All of them offer excellent Italian dishes consisting of pastas, pizzas, vegetable salads, pastries and ice creams. **Pizza Mizza** is the cosy place in the lane behind the Comenius University. One of the best pizzerias in Bratislava is **Restaurant Corleone** where also other meals are served apart from pizzas. The **Pizza House** is nearby. Its offer is good and the courteous waiters certainly contribute to client's satisfaction. The typical Italian restaurant **La Trattoria** in the Old Town serves sea fish and a rich choice of light Italian wines apart from pastas and pizzas.

Coffee and teahouses
The coffeehouses of Bratislava attract with their comfort and intimate atmosphere. Many of them enjoy a long tradition and were visited by famous figures in the past. The former legendary coffeehouses like **Grand, Astorka, Múzejka, Štefánka, Tatra** or **Alžbetka** are still opened and their service reached a good European level. All of them also offer cakes, pastries, sandwiches or even complete meals.

Lovers of sweets and cakes should drop in the establishments in the Viennese style - **Kaffe Mayer** or **Rolland caffe** on the Hlavné námestie square. The **Piano bar** in the town centre is furnished in the style of the 1930s. Some guests find its artistic flair with jazz music especially pleasant. **U anjelov** is another establishment that falls in the category of what is considered an ideal coffeehouse.

Those who want to make use of the Internet or computer service should visit the **C@fé Online** which occupies two floors of a remarkable building built

Pizzerias

Pizza Mizza
Tobrucká 5
☎ 5296 5034

Restaurant Corleone
Hviezdoslavovo nám. 21
☎ 5443 5548

Pizza House
Hviezdoslavovo nám. 15
☎ 5443 1840

La Trattoria
Ferienčíková 13
☎ 5296 1620

Pizzeria No 33
Obchodná 33
☎ 5273 3710

Ramazzotti
Vysoká 15
☎ 5293 1312

Pizza Hut
Drevená 8
☎ 5441 0488

Coffee and teahouses

Kaffe Mayer
Hlavné nám. 4
☎ 5441 1741

Rolland caffé
Hlavné nám. 5
☎ 5443 1372

Piano Bar
Laurinská 11
☎ 5441 5880

U anjelov
Laurinská 19
☎ 5443 2724

C@fé Online
Obchodná 48

Jazz Café
Ventúrska 5
☎ 5443 4661

Café Ister
Ventúrska 8
☎ 5443 5874

Atrium
Gorkého 3
☎ 5960 3348

Čajovňa Pohoda
Laurinská 3
☎ 5443 3103

Čajovňa v galérii
Michalský dvor
Michalská 3

Čajovňa
Zámocká 18
☎ 0902 356 065

Wine cellars

Kláštorná vináreň
Františkánska 2
☎ 5443 0430

Veľkí františkáni
Františkánske nám. 10
☎ 5443 3073

Šenkvická viecha
Panenská 35

Bakchus
Hlboká 5
☎ 5249 4178

Sv. Urban
Klobučnícka 4
☎ 5443 2537

in the cubist style with fifty computers available for its guests. Jazz music offered in **Jazz café**, which also has its own gallery and in the night it changes into a genuine jazz club with live band and an excellent atmosphere. Recently, several teahouses sprang in Bratislava, one of them called Pohoda offers an especially comfortable and nice time for a cup of tea.

Wine cellars

A good meal calls for a good wine. The viticultural tradition of Bratislava roots in the Roman times. Excellent wines were produced here since time immemorial and the wine cellars of Bratislava, which were originally parts of households, are famous. The old cellars do not exist now but the good wine of the grapes grown on the sunny slopes of the Little Carpathian mountains are still sold in Bratislava's wine cellars. One of the is **Kláštorná vináreň** which seats in the typical cellars below an old monastery and apart from good domestic wines it also serves food. The **Veľkí františkáni** is visited above all by youth and the students love to sit at the **Šenkvická viecha** where they can take tasty soups and all kinds of titbits accompanied by red or white wines.

Pubs

Beer is perhaps the most sought after and popular beverage of Slovaks, the same as Czechs, and it is tapped in numerous pubs all over the city. The newly established **Eden pub** won great popularity; it also serves meals. The striking furniture of the **Irish pub**, its unique atmosphere and the offer of typical Irish meals and beers is undoubtedly the most popular pub of Bratislava and it is always full of native and foreign fans of beer.

In contrast, the **1. Slovak pub** is furnished in a typical Slovak style. Each of its eleven rooms is different and represents a certain part of the Slovak history and reality. Its capacity is 600 seats. It offers special prices for students

Shopping

The purchase power of people of Bratislava is the highest in Slovakia. Maybe this is the reason why there are so many shopping opportunities here including large departments stores, hyper- or supermarkets and a great amount of small sometimes smart and exclusive shops. Bratislava though is in no way a cheap place. Most of people economise and do their shopping after seasons, it time of sale at reduced prices.

The shopping "paradise" of the Old Town concentrates around the Obchodná, Michalská, and Laurinská ulica Streets. There also are several market places where goods of all kinds are sold – starting by fresh vegetable and fruit and ending by hand-made artefacts or clothes. Generally, the shops open from Monday to Friday from 9:00 to 6 p.m.and on Saturday when they close at midday. But of course, there are commercial establishments, which open throughout the week while some of the largest shopping

Pubs

Varadero
Obchodná 42
☎ 5273 1350

Irish pub
Sedlárska 6
☎ 5441 0706

Umelka Pub
Dostojevského rad 2
☎ 5263 4754

1. Slovak pub
Obchodná 62
☎ 5292 6367

El Diablo Bar
Sedlárska 6
☎ 0904 556 886

Eden pub
Obchodná 48
☎ 5273 1253

Chicago 30´s Club
Nám. SNP 8
☎ 0907 108 628

KGB
Krčma gurmánov
Obchodná 52
☎ 5273 1278

Česká pivnica
Radlinského 39
☎ 5249 1945

Koník pub
Mlynské Nivy 24
☎ 5263 4527

112

Antiquities

Art Decoration
Kozia 15
☎ 5441 2370

Antiques Hasíková
Michalská 3
☎ 5443 1578

Books

Svet knihy
Obchodná 4
☎ 5464 8837

Pištek
Obchodná 2
☎ 5464 0814

Art Fórum
Kozia 20
☎ 5441 1898

Big Ben Book Shop
Michalská 1

La Reduta
Palackého 2
☎ 5443 0203

Slovenský spisovateľ
Laurinská 2
☎ 5443 3760

Antikvariát Steiner
Ventúrska 20
☎ 5443 3778

centres open even round the clock.

Antiquities
The collectors of antiquities can please themselves and pursue their hobby by visiting several antiquity shops concentrated above all in the Old Town. They

include the shops like **Art Decoration** or **Antiques Hasíková** where remarkable objects, paintings, and precious trifles in different historic styles are available.

Gifts and souvernirs
Those visitors of Bratislava who like to see hand-made folk artistic or artisan products, gifts or souvenirs such as puppets, wood carved objects, embroidery, leather goods should visit the shops **Folk Folk** or **ÚĽUV** in the city centre. Domestic wines can be also bought in specialised shops. There are small shops all over the city selling innovative, original specific or typical objects of domestic and imported produce to carry away as a commemorative object or gift.

Books

Bookshops are many in Bratislava and the most interesting and well-supplied are of course in the city centre. There also are several shops selling literature in foreign languages. The largest bookshops are **Svet Knihy**, **Pištek** on the Obchodná ulica St.. **Art Fórum** and **Gump** are the most favourite for its alternative and specific orientation. **Big Ben Bookshop** is focused on English books. Old and rare books are sold at **Antikvariát Steiner**.

Shopping centres

Everything under one roof and the widest assortment of goods is offered by modern department stores and shopping centres. Their number is constantly increasing and they are now built in the suburban zones. Tesco and Dunaj are the best known among the centric shopping centres. The City Center is the name of a new smart shop in the Obchodná ulica St. It sells modern goods with excellent quality. Large hypermarkets such as **Aupark** in the quarter of Petržalka, **Polus City Center** and **Shopping Palace** in the east are those situated in the periphery of Bratislava.

Markets

Markets offer a special atmosphere full of colours, sounds, forms and smells.

Gifts and souvernirs

Folk Folk
Obchodná 10
☎ 5443 4292
Rybárska brána 2
☎ 5443 4874

ÚĽUV
Michalská 4
☎ 5443 2288
Nám. SNP 12
☎ 5292 3802

Bratislava SHOP
Nám. SNP 13
☎ 5926 5561

Shopping centres

Tesco
Kamenné nám. 1
Lamač
Petržalka
Zlaté piesky

Dunaj
Nám. SNP 30

City Center
Obchodná 58

Aupark
Einsteinova 18
☎ 6826 6200

Polus City Center
Vajnorská 100
☎ 4444 1234

Shopping Palace
Zlaté piesky

Danubia
Panónska cesta 16
☎ 6820 8808

For instance, the recently reconstructed town market hall referred to as **Stará tržnica** is in the very centre of the town and it offers all that a genuine market should have: fresh fruit and vegetable, flowers and souvenirs.

Entertainment

Bratislava does not have what might be called purely entertaining zones. In spite of it there are places where to go in search of fun. There are two centres outside the Old Town: the **Polus City Center** and **Aupark**, which are gaining increasing popularity. They are in fact shopping complexes but they also have several cinemas, theatres, etc. The topical programmes of cinemas or theatres are published in most dailies and the tickets can be purchased directly in the establishments or through Internet.

Theatres
Compared to its size, Bratislava has many theatres. Most of them are in the city centre and the theatre season is from September to June. The theatres normally close during summer and the plays staged in open air, on courtyards or squares take over the role of theatres. Most of the performances start at 19:00 and normally are sold out – so it is advisable to buy the tickets well in advance. The local

Divadlo a.ha
Školská 14
☎ 5249 6822

Radošinské naivné
divadlo
Škultétyho 5
☎ 5556 3508

**Concerts, opera
and ballet**

Slovenské národné
divadlo – opera a balet
Hviezdoslavovo nám. 1
☎ 5443 3890

Slovenská filharmónia
Reduta, Palackého 2
☎ 5443 5242

Slovenský rozhlas
Mýtna 1
☎ 5727 3111

Moyzesova sieň
Vajanského nábr. 12
☎ 5292 5347

Hudobné centrum
Mirbachov palác
Františkánske nám. 11
☎ 5443 1556

Hudobná sieň
Bratislavského hradu
Mudroňova 1
☎ 5441 3349

Koncertná sieň Klarisky
Uršulínska 11
☎ 5441 6548

actors act on the stages of the Slovak National Theatre, which comprises the **Divadlo P. O. Hviezdoslava** and **Malá scéna**. The **Astorka Korzo 90** and **Štúdio L & S** are small and rather intellectual scenes while the Divadlo West stages plays and musicals with the touch of commerciality.

Concerts, opera and ballet

Bratislava is also referred to sometimes as a "city of music". The musical life of Slovakia concentrates in its **National Theatre** and as there is a great demand for tickets they are always sold out. The Opera of Bratislava is much visited for the quality of its singers, which also attracts the audience of Vienna and Austria in general. The names like P. Dvorský, Ľ. Rybárska or M. Babjak are the guarantee of an indeed decent level of the local opera performances.

The majority of operas are sung in original languages in order to give chance to foreigners to enjoy them. In the vicinity of the Opera House is the concert hall of the **Slovak Philharmonic Orchestra** – the Reduta House. Musicals and lighter genres are typical for the **Nová scéna** theatre. Jazz concerts held on Tuesdays and Thursdays can be listened to in the **Jazz-Avi Club**. Every autumn Bratislava lives its international festival of music: The Jazz Days of Bratislava. International festival of classic music is also organised in Bratislava (Music Festival of Bratislava) every autumn.

Cinemas

The biggest cinemas are normally in shopping areas such as **Polus City Center** and **Aupark** rather out of town. They mostly offer Hollywood films

Discoteques and nightclubs

Jalta bar
Gorkého 15

U-Club
Nábr. arm. gen. L. Svobodu

Cirkus Barok
Rázusovo nábr.
☎ 5464 2091

Woch Music Club
Františkánske nám. 7
☎ 5443 2928

Laverna 1224
Nám. SNP 11

Harley-Davidson Saloon
Rebarborová 1/a
☎ 4319 1094, 95

Live! Club
Aupark, Einsteinova 18
☎ 6345 4108

Duna Music Club
Radlinského 11

Casinos

Kasíno Park
Hviezdoslavovo nám. 21

Casino Café Reduta
Mostová 3
☎ 5443 2021

and the films for more demanding audience are available in smaller cinemas in the interior of the city. The daily press provides detailed information on the topical programmes of the individual cinemas.

Discoteques and nightclubs

Although the nightlife of the Slovak metropolis is not so rich as that of other European capitals there are establishments where the life starts at midnight and continues until the next morning. The best known and the oldest night bar is the **Jalta bar** that also offers female and male striptease. The clubs which are much visited for good house parties sometimes led by famous DJs is the **U-Club**, **Cirkus Barok** at the Danube embankment or **Woch Music Club** in the centre. The discoteque **Laverna 1224** is situated next to the Old Market Hal and the nightclubs a bit retired from the centre such as **Live! Club** in Aupark or **Harley-Davidson Saloon** are preferred above all by the youth.

Casinos
Those who like to play American or French roulette, black jack or other plays can visit one of the casinos of Bratislava. They are situated in **Reduta** or **Kasíno Park**, a smaller and more intimate one is in the Crowne Plaza Hotel.

Museums and galleries

City Museum
Primaciálne nám. 3
☎ 5443 4742
www.muzeumbratislava.sk

Expositions:
Exposition of the history of Bratislava
Old City Hall
Primaciálne nám. 1
☎ 5920 5130
◎ Tue-Fri 10 a.m.-5 p.m.,
Sat-Sun 11 a.m.-6 p.m.

Exposition of Viticulture
Apponyi Palace
Radničná 1
☎ 5920 5141
◎ Tue-Fri 10 a.m.-5 p.m.,
Sat-Sun 11 a.m.-6 p.m.,
Oct-Apr Tue-Sun 9.30 a.m.-4.30 p.m.

Exposition of arts and crafts
Beblavého 1
☎ 5441 2784
◎ Tue-Fri 10 a.m.-5 p.m.,
Sat-Sun 11 a.m.-6 p.m.,
Oct-Apr Tue-Sun 9.30 a.m.-4.30 p.m.

Exposition of weapons and town fortifications
Michalská veža tower
Michalská 24, ☎ 5443 3044
◎ Tue-Fri 10 a.m.-5 p.m.,
Sat-Sun 11 a.m.-6 p.m.,
Oct-Apr 9.30 a.m.-4.30 p.m.

Exposition of historical watches
The House of the Good Shepherd
Židovská 1
☎ 5441 1940
◎ Mon-Fri 10 a.m.-5 p.m.,
Sat-Sun 10 a.m.-6 p.m.,
Oct-Apr Tue-Sun 9.30 a.m.-4.30 p.m.

The castle Devín
Muránska ulica
☎ 6573 0105
◎ May-Sep Tue-Fri 10 a.m.-5 p.m.,
Sat-Sun 10 a.m.-6 p.m.

Music exposition
The house of J. N. Hummel
Klobučnícka 2
☎ 5443 3888
◎ Mon-Fri 10 a.m.-6 p.m.,
Sat-Sun 10 a.m.-2 p.m.

Museum of Antique, Gerulata
Gerulatská 69
☎ 6285 9332
◎ May-Sep Tue-Sun 10 a.m.-5 p.m.

Museum of Arthur Fleischmann
Biela 6
◎ Tue-Fri 10 a.m.-5 p.m.
Sat-Sun 11 a.m.-6 p.m.,
Oct-Apr 9.30 a.m.-4.30 p.m.

Slovak national museum
Vajanského nábr. 2
☎ 5934 9141
www.snm.sk

Expositions:
Museum of Natural Science
Vajanského nábr. 2
☎ 5934 9122
◎ Tue-Sun 9 a.m.-5 p.m.

Archeological Museum
Žižkova 12
☎ 5441 6034
◎ Tue-Sun 9 a.m.-5 p.m.

Historical Museum
Castle
☎ 5441 1444
◎ Tue-Sun 9 a.m.-5 p.m.

Music Museum
Castle
☎ 5441 3349
◎ Tue-Sun 9 a.m.-5 p.m.

Museum of Jewish Culture
Zsigray's curia
Židovská 17
☎ 5441 1444, 5934 9142
☺ Mon-Sun 11 a.m.-5 p.m.

Mausoleum of Chatam Sófer
Nábr. arm. gen. L. Svobodu
☎ 0903 265 453

Transport Museum
Šancová 1
☎ 5244 4163
☺ Tue-Fri 10 a.m.-5 p.m., Sat-Sun 9 a.m.-6 p.m.

Museum of Police SR
Gunduličova 2
☎ 5296 1136
☺ Tue-Sat 10 a.m.-5 p.m.

Museum of Commerce
Linzbothova 16
☎ 4552 7268

Slovak National Gallery

Water Barracks
Rázusovo nábr. 2
☎ 5443 2082
☺ Tue-Sun 10 a.m.-6 p.m.

Esterházy Palace
Štúrovo nám. 4, ☎ 5443 2081
☺ Tue-Sun 10 a.m.-6 p.m.

Gallery of Bratislava

Primatial Palace
Primaciálne nám. 1
☎ 5935 6111
☺ Tue-Sun 11 a.m.-5 p.m.

Mirbach Palace
Františkánske nám. 11
☎ 5443 1556
☺ Tue-Sun 11 a.m.-6 p.m.

Pálffy Palace
Panská 19
☎ 5443 3627
☺ Tue-Sun 11 a.m.-6 p.m.

Gallery Ardan
Dobrovičova 7
☎ 0905 443 106, 5249 3235
☺ Tue-Fri 10 a.m.-6 p.m.,
Sat 10 a.m.-4 p.m.

Gallery Artotéka
Kapucínska 1
☺ Mon, Wen, Thu 1 p.m.-5.30 p.m.,
Tue, Fri 1.30 p.m.-4 p.m.

Buryzone
Čajakova 11
☎ 5244 4559
www.buryzone.sk
☺ Wen-Thu 2 p.m.-10 p.m.,
Fri 7 p.m.-12 p.m.

**Danubiana Meulensteen
Art Museum**
Bratislava-Čunovo
☎ 0903 605 505
www.danubiana.sk
☺ May-Sep 10 a.m.-8 p.m.,
Oct-Apr 10 a.m.-6 p.m.

Gallery Donner
Klobučnícka 4
☎ 5443 3753

Divyd
Klobučnícka 2
☎ 5443 3888
www.divyd.sk

Gallery F7
Františkánske nám. 7
☺ Tue-Sun 1 p.m.-6 p.m.

Gallery of Slovenská poisťovňa
Dostojevského rad 28
☎ 5963 1111
☺ Mon-Fri 8 a.m.-4 p.m.

Gallery of Slovenská sporiteľňa
Zelená 2,
☎ 5977 2312, 5443 1491
◑ Mon-Fri 8 a.m.-4 p.m.

Gallery SFPA
Panenská 33, ☎ 5443 3155
◑ Mon-Fri 9 a.m.-5 p.m.

Gallery SPP
Drevená 4, ☎ 5413 1251
◑ Tue-Sun 10 a.m.-6 p.m.

GALLERY X
Zámočnícka 5
◑ Mon-Fri 1 p.m.-6 p.m.,
Sat 1 p.m.-5 p.m.

Gallery Z
Zichy Palace
Ventúrska 9, ☎ 0903 468 776
www.hulik.sk
◑ Mon-Sat 12 a.m.-6 p.m.

Gallery HIT
Hviezdoslavo nám.18
☎ 0908 790 942
www.galeriahit.com
◑ Tue-Fri 3 p.m.-7 p.m.

K. Gallery
Ventúrska 8, ☎ 5443 3927
◑ Mon-Fri 1 p.m.-6 p.m.

K. F. A. Gallery
Karpatská 11, ☎ 5249 7030
www.kfa.sk
◑ Mon-Fri 8.30 a.m.-4.30 p.m.

Gallery Komart
Zámočnícka 8, ☎ 5441 2918
www.galeriakomart.sk

Gallery Marat Art
Panská 6, ☎ 5443 4689

Gallery Michalský dvor
Michalská 3, ☎ 5441 1079

www.gallery.sk
◑ Tue-Sun 1 p.m.-6 p.m.

Miro Gallery
Košická 56, ☎ 5070 2866-8
◑ Mon-Fri 11 a.m.-5 p.m.,
Sat 9 a.m.-1 p.m.

Gallery Médium
Hviezdoslavovo nám. 18
☎ 5443 5334
www.vsvu.sk/medium/galeria
◑ Mon-Fri 10 a.m.-5 p.m.,
Sat 10 a.m.-4 p.m.

Gallery Nova
Baštová 2, ☎ 5443 3039
www.galeria-nova.sk
◑ Tue-Sun 13.00-18.00

Open Gallery
Baštová 5, ☎ 5441 3316
www.scca.sk
◑ Mon-Fri 1 p.m.-6 p.m.

Gallery Profil
Prepoštská 4, ☎ 5443 0459
www.fotofo.sk
◑ Tue-Sun 1 p.m.-6 p.m.

Gallery SAS
Panská 15, ☎ 5441 8607
www.archinet.sk

Soga Gallery
Panská 4, ☎ 5464 9942-3
www.soga.sk
◑ Mon- Fri 10 a.m.-6 p.m.,
Sat 10 a.m.-1 p.m.

T Gallery
Panská 24 ☎ 0903 601 656
www.tgallery.sk
◑ Mon-Sun 10 a.m.-6 p.m.

ÚĽUV
Dobrovičova, ☎ 5296 4153
www.uluv.sk

REGISTER

The most interesting destinations of tourists:

*   interesting
**   very interesting
***   extra interesting
**** top interesting

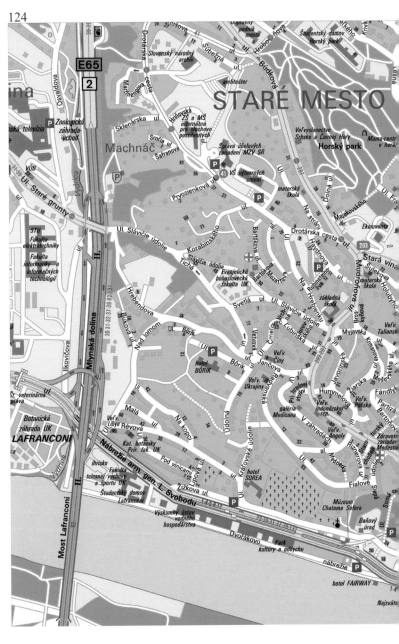

Výskumný ústav vinohradnícky a vinársky
Výskumný kontrolný a skúšobný ústav pôľnohospodársky
hotel GALÉRIA
Matúškova
Ul. Jaskovy rad
Záchranná a dopravná zdravotnícka služba
Združená hotelová akadémia
ihrisko
Radlinského
komunálna banka
Danubius Elektrik
Radlinského nárocie divadlo
Umelecké a kongresové centrum ISTROPOLIS
Trnav mýto

Bratislava hlavná stanica
Štátny ústav na kontrolu liečiv
Predstaničné nám.
Poľná
Dobšinského
Šrádkárska škola
Špeciálna zákl. škola
Beskydská
Karpatská ul.
Račianske mýto
Šancová
Račianska ul.
tržnica
VUB
Múzeum dopravy
Železničná
SR
Bukurešťská ul.
Holekova
ul. I. II.
Mýtna ul.
I. Legionárska
Železničná nem.
Kováčiková ska
Slovakia UniBanka
CSOB

I. II. Šancová
Povraznícka
Ministerstvo financií
Belopotocká
CSOB
STU Elektrotech fakulta
Bernolákova
Stud. domov J. Hronca
Wilsonova
Stud. domov N. Belojanisa
Slov. spor.

Štefánikova
Národná banka Slovenska
Miestne u P. Márie kultúrne
Vazovova
Nám. M. Benku
Kmeťovo nám ul.
Stredná geodetická škola

Slovenský rozhlas
Ministerstvo dopravy pôšt a telekomu
základná škola gymnázium
Kostol Nanebovzatie
Floriánska nám.
Krížna ul.
Záhradnícka
Justičný palác
OLO
UniB

slobody WC
Slovenská
Starohorská
Blumentálska
Pedagogická fakulta UK
Kocelo
Bazová

Fak. architektúry STU
Mýtna ul.
Slovenská technická univerzita
Fakultná nám.
Odborárske nám.
Moskovská
Strážnická
Sasinkova
CU
Společ dom
Veletr

Úrad vlády SR
Jozefská
kino HVIEZDA
hotel TATRA
Slovanská
Americké nám.
Lekárska fakulta UK
Slov. ped. nakl.
Okresné riaditeľstvo PZ
Skladištná Istrobr

Prezidentský palác
Kollárovo nám.
Nová scéna
Mickiewiczova
OTF
Stredisko cenných papierov
Ul. Tatra banka
Medická záhrada
Polná

Hodžovo nám.
Vysoká
Ľudová banka
Slovenská spor.
Marianska
Vyššia voj. správa Územná voj. správa 1, 3, 4. Dobrov.
základná francúzsku škola
Ondrejský cintorín
Budovateľská

Tatracentrum
synagóga
Holienkova
Ministerstvo práce soc. veci a rodiny
VUB
Ľudová banka
VUB

hotel FORUM
VUB
Onkolog. ústav sv. Alžbety
kino CHARLES
NsP
Ferienčíkova
Ministerstvo vnútra
Veľv. Egypta

PKB
kalvínsky kostol
Heydukova
Cintorínska
hotel KYJEV
Autob Mlyns

Hurbanovo nám.
hotel SLOFA
Nám.
gymnázium základná škola
Kablo

Div SNP
ASTORKA
KORZO'90
WEST
TESCO
Šancová
Dunajská
Slov. film. ústav
Štátne bábkové divadlo
divadlo
základná škola
Chemika

Zámoc. Michalská
Bela
Hlavné nám.
Kamenné nám.
Tatra banka
Slov. banka
Tatra banka
Tovarenská
Tatra banka
Elektrovod

Magistrát
Primaciálne nám.
Gorkého
Nedbalova
Grösslingova
Gen. prokur. Akad. vzdel.
Radničná
Dom zahraničných Slovákov

Gal. mesta
Gal. Médium
Hviezdoslavovo nám.
Panská
Sedlárska
Rybárska brána
Zelená
Komenského nám.
Galova
Jakubovo nám.
Ministerstvo pôdohosp.

OTP banka
Reduta
SNK
gymnázium
Šienke nem.
PKB
divadlo STOKA

Slovenská národná galéria
Palackého
Medená
Tobrucká
Šafárikovo nám.
Dostojevského ul.
Pribinova ul.
SND (vo výstavbe)
TA SR

Ľudová banka
Vajanského nábr.
Fajnorovo nábr.
Ministerstvo vnútra SR
Pribinova
Dom lodníkov Slovnaft

hotel DEVÍN
hotel GRÁCIA
Slov. plavba a prístavu
Lodná osobná doprava
Mýtny domček
Galéria Minislovensko
Landererova ul.

1 Muzeání ul.
2 Prešovská ul.

THE MAPS YOU NEED

VEĽKÝ AUTOATLAS
SLOVENSKA
1 : 100 000

A EURÓPY
1 : 1 000 000

127
MALÉ KARPATY
BRATISLAVA
1 : 50 000

GPS

TURISTICKÁ MAPA
WANDERKARTE • HIKING MAP • TURISTIKÉRKÉP
MAPA TURYSTYCZNA
4. VYDANIE

7
RADFAHRKARTE
CYCLIST'S MAP
KERÉKPÁRTURISZTIKAI TÉRKÉP

PODROBNÁ
CYKLOTURISTICKÁ MAPA
1 : 100 000

BRATISLAVA
PODUNAJSKO
• výškové profily trás
• praktické informácie
• cykloturistický sprievodca
2. VYDANIE

BRATISLAVA
1 : 15 000

MAPA MESTA
TOWN PLAN • STADTPLAN
PLAN MIASTA • VÁROSTÉRKÉP

ORTOFOTOMAPA

BRATISLAVA
GEODIS

PODROBNÝ TURISTICKÝ ATLAS
1 : 25 000
MALÉ
KARPATY

1. VYDANIE

BRATISLAVA
MAPA MESTA
TOWN PLAN • STADTPLAN • PLAN MIASTA
• VÁROSTÉRKÉP

mapa mesta 1 : 10 000
mapa okolia Bratislavy 1 : 100 000
linky mestskej hromadnej dopravy
dôležité a praktické informácie
register ulíc a námestí
4. VYDANIE

ATLAS TURISTICKÝCH ZAUJÍMAVOSTÍ
BRATISLAVA
• PODUNAJSKO
1 : 100 000

1. VYDANIE

VKÚ, akciová spoločnosť
976 03 HARMANEC 13
Slovak Republic

tel.: 00421/48/ 419 85 14
fax: 00421/48/ 419 83 38

e-mail: predaj@vku.sk
http://www.vkuslovakia.com